SUCCESSFUL HOMESCHOOLING MADE EASY

DISCLAIMER AND/OR LEGAL NOTICES:

The author of this book has attempted to make the information as accurate as possible. However, the information in this book is for personal educational use only and is provided in good faith without any express or implied warranty. The author has provided book titles as a service to readers. This service does not mean that the author wholeheartedly endorses those in books any way.

This edition published in 2021 by
Living Book Press
www.livingbookpress.com
ISBN: 978-1-922348-78-4
© 2020 Stephanie Walmsley

All rights reserved. No part of this publication may be reproduced, stored in a retrieval system, or transmitted in any other form or means—electronic, mechanical, photocopying, recording or otherwise, without the prior permission of the copyright owner and the publisher or as provided by Australian law.

A catalogue record for this book is available from the National Library of Australia

successful homeschooling MADE EASY

BY STEPHANIE WALMSLEY

www.SuccessfulHomeSchoolingMadeEasy.com

CONTENTS

	INTRODUCTION	1
1.	MY HOMESCHOOL STORY	3
2.	START HOMESCHOOLING TODAY	6
3.	MATHEMATICS MADE EASY	18
4.	WELCOME HOME!	26
5.	FIREPROOF YOUR HOMESCHOOL	37
6.	THREE QUESTIONS ...	44
7.	FULFIL YOUR DREAMS	48
8.	WHY CURRICULUM DOESN'T MATTER	53
9.	YOU MIGHT NEED TO LET GO OF THE GOOD THINGS	60
10.	HOUSEWORK AND HOMESCHOOL	66
11.	MAKE A FULL TIMETABLE	74
12.	RECORD KEEPING THE EASY WAY	82
13.	EBB AND FLOW	91
14.	MAKE YOUR LIBRARY VISIT COUNT	97
15.	HOW TO WRITE A LESSON PLAN	104
16.	TEACH SCIENCE	109
17.	AVOIDING STRESS AND BURNOUT	115
18.	WHAT WOULD YOU DO DIFFERENTLY?	121
19.	WIN THE CLUTTER WAR	129
20.	KEEP YOUR FAMILY SAFE ONLINE	137
21.	ARE YOU ON THE ROAD TO SUCCESS?	146
22.	TWEAK AND IMPROVE	152
23.	START AND END IN A SPECIAL WAY	159
24.	LOOK HOW FAR YOU'VE COME!	163
	ABOUT THE AUTHOR	166

INTRODUCTION

> *There is not the slightest doubt in my mind that you can succeed in homeschooling.*

Homeschooling is a marvellous way of life. It's a wonderful way to bring up your children, and I am keen to help you enjoy this lifestyle of home learning with your children.

I can show you how you can start homeschooling your children straight away, and how it can be fun for everyone involved, including you.

One happy aspect of homeschooling is that you will find that you yourself will learn and become educated on so many subjects, and that's a great feeling. And it feels so good to see your children developing a love of learning themselves.

Another aspect that can be overwhelming, is that you will also find that you are being constantly bombarded with interesting and good curriculum, books, websites, and equipment, so that it's easy to become overwhelmed and burned out.

That's where this book will help you. I want to 'fireproof' you against those things and I want to help you discover and apply the homeschooling way that will best suit you and your family. So that you are enjoying daily life with the family.

In many ways this is more than a book on homeschooling; it's more of a manual for homeschooling and family life in general. It's all about how to live and enjoy the full life of homeschooling your children.

I am confident that if you are reading this book, you are going to be able to enjoy homeschooling. In fact, there is not the slightest doubt in my mind that you can succeed in homeschooling. I will give you the tools, and if you use all the tools, I know you WILL succeed.

In this book I'll show you how to:
- Homeschool successfully and happily.
- Make a timetable that works.
- Fit in a wide variety of subjects in teaching your child.

- Balance homeschooling and housework, completing all you need to do in a timely way.
- Homeschool your child, whether a pre-schooler or highschooler.
- Homeschool a group of children of different ages.
- Make good choices of what will suit your children and family when choosing curriculum and books.
- Sidestep homeschool stress and homeschool burnout.

HOW TO GET THE BEST OUT OF THIS BOOK

Each chapter in the book builds on the previous ones, so the best thing to do is to read the book from front to back. To begin with, I will show you how to ease into homeschooling in a simple way. If you are already homeschooling, you might like to look at this chapter to see if it offers any clues to an easier daily life for you.

As the chapters build up you will see how to add a new subject to your timetable for the first eight weeks, and at the same time that you are doing that, you are digging deep to discover the best approach to homeschooling for you personally.

I recommend that you work on a chapter a week, and you will find that each chapter concludes with a weekly assignment. This is a small task to help you apply what you are learning, and hopefully it will enrich your life as you apply it.

After eight weeks I will help you build a new and improved timetable, and then we will go deeper and wider to look at various aspects of homeschooling and family life.

As you read, you will see that there are some helpful charts and forms, and these are all available to you online. You can then print what you need for your own homeschool folder.

A NOTEBOOK IS A GOOD IDEA

You might like to get yourself a notebook or loose-leaf folder to store your notes as you work through the book. And if this is your own personal copy of the book, then do what C. S. Lewis suggested, and write notes and messages to yourself in the margins, highlight parts you like, and generally make the book your own.

Let me start by introducing myself to you and telling you about my own homeschooling experience.

CHAPTER 1
MY HOMESCHOOL STORY

We first started officially homeschooling many years ago, in early 1985 when our oldest child was almost six. Homeschooling was very different then—in fact we homeschooled for quite a while without meeting or knowing a single family who was homeschooling, and our own families thought we were 'going through a phase'. Nobody around us had heard of the term *homeschooling* at that time. There was no homeschooling curriculum available to me, so I made up my own curriculum and scoured the bookshops for books to fit what I wanted to do.

As I had been a primary school teacher, it wasn't too hard. And the best thing was that I had been mentored by an old-fashioned-style senior teacher; I learned so much from her about the basics of what I think of as *real teaching* and *real learning*.

After three years training to be a teacher I had been given my piece of paper saying that I was qualified to teach. I had learnt heaps about the sociology, history, psychology, and pedagogy of teaching. I had done very well during my practices in schools with real life children to teach. But I knew remarkably little about actual classroom teaching. Looking back, I am surprised and just a tad concerned that we were let loose in the classroom.

My Head of Department was very generous in teaching me how to teach. She knew what she wanted from the children and she explained it to me quickly. I obeyed her very well, and I got the good results she was after, so that pleased us both.

Then, as a homeschooling mum, I used my teaching experience to homeschool and it worked. I soon developed my own style which improved as I became more experienced as a parent and a homeschooler. I got some things right and plenty wrong. But my philosophy stayed the same, while my method of applying that philosophy improved and became more refined and streamlined.

The two older children had some time in school. Then they came home again and joined their younger sister in homeschooling. After a while we started meeting others who were starting out on their own homeschooling adventure and I started a homeschool support group.

Having homeschooling friends was fun, although it also made things harder for us to homeschool in some ways. For example, one of the things that I didn't bother with when we knew no other homeschoolers, was working in with school holidays. We ignored school holidays and just took rests and breaks when people were tired, then we started back with more formal learning when we had rested. But socialising with other homeschoolers and working in with extra-curricular activities meant that it was very hard to keep up this relaxed approach.

Another thing I noticed was the developing homeschool market, mainly from overseas, having a strong influence on homeschoolers in New Zealand. Over time, I saw that there were 'fashions' in homeschooling. For example, a certain mathematics programme or writing programme or history or science programme would become fashionable. It felt like too many people were going for the fashionable programme rather than what their children needed. It's never a good idea to get distracted with beautiful tools is it? It's always best to focus on what your child needs at the moment.

Over the years, homeschooling has become more popular and widely accepted. I haven't been surprised by this because it's such a happy lifestyle; it's a great way to spend time with your children; and you can be confident that your child is getting a good, wholesome, balanced education.

The internet has made knowledge and information more accessible too, so that was another big change and benefit for homeschoolers. But there is a down-side to the internet. I started to see that homeschoolers were feeling stressed and unhappy. They had so much information available, but it seemed to be confusing rather than helping them. I saw that they were spending a lot of money on equipment, curriculum and classes that were good for some people, but not necessarily good for them.

I could see how hard it was for people to identify what was the best for their family and what was better to leave for others.

Homeschooling had become an expensive and worrying lifestyle for many families.

Of course, the support of an experienced homeschooling friend can make all the difference to a homeschooler. And that's what I want this book to be for you. I can take you logically, calmly, and simply through some basic steps to help you plan your own homeschooling style and method. And as you read, I hope you will learn how to live the life that *you* want with *your* children.

CHAPTER 2
START HOMESCHOOLING TODAY

> *A journey of a thousand miles begins with a single step.*

For many of us, the thought of homeschooling your child can be daunting, and it can feel like an immense responsibility. Most people wonder where to start, and they are certainly afraid of getting it wrong. Then there's the question of how you will manage as your child gets older. And what do you say to those who ask you about exams, university and a million other things?

Those are all valid concerns and questions. But we'll start small. Let's concentrate on *this week* with your child, and how to start homeschooling *today*.

First, I will give you an overview of homeschooling and enough information to apply in your home with your family. Then you will actually be able to say that you have started homeschooling.

Over the next following chapters I will take you deep on various topics so that you can accurately work out the way you are going to homeschool.

We'll start with a plan for the next two months. This will be a timetable that will cover your first eight weeks of homeschooling. By working in this way, you will ensure that you will be successful in homeschooling in the *long run*. You *won't* suffer from burnout, you *will* enjoy homeschooling. And you *will* succeed and see good progress with your children.

FIRST MAKE A TIMETABLE

No matter what style of homeschooling you choose, you will need a timetable. Some people might think that unschoolers don't need a timetable. But you will find that even successful unschoolers have some sort of timetable. It may be flexible, and fluid, but it will be there.

This step of making a timetable is crucial to your well-being and peace of mind. It will help you be a successful homeschooler.

So let's start with your timetable. This timetable will last you for eight weeks. It is your Eight Week Timetable.

The reason for having a timetable for only eight weeks is so that you can start homeschooling today in a simple way, and at the same time you can start to develop your ideas and vision about homeschooling long term. At the end of the eight weeks you will be ready to make a new timetable and I will show you how.

The new timetable will cover things in more depth, and you may be tempted to skip the *Eight Week Timetable* and rush straight off to the more detailed timetable. DON'T DO IT. You want to make a good job of homeschooling. This is the way to do that. Your *Eight Week Timetable* is a wonderful timetable for your first eight weeks. It's simple, it's easy to do and you will be able to relax, knowing that you are teaching your children, that you are making progress, and also, most importantly, that you are building up a very clear idea of what you want to achieve in the long run.

To start preparing to make your timetable, I have some questions for you. Give your very honest answers to these questions. It's not a test, and there are no right or wrong answers. This will help you plan a timetable which will actually work for you. You can use your notebook or folder to keep these answers in. We will be building up pages over the course of the book.

> *'If you don't know where you are going, how can you expect to get there?'*
>
> BASIL S. WALSH

EIGHT WEEK TIMETABLE **PLANNING QUESTIONS**

1. What time does your family normally get up on a weekday morning? Say what's comfortable at the moment, and not what you would like it to be.
2. Make a list of the morning chores that you have at your house. It might include things like: get dressed, make the bed, eat breakfast, wash the dishes, put washing in the washing machine, sweep the floor, feed the animals... Make your own list.

3. Do you and your children concentrate better for academic work in the morning or in the afternoon?
4. Do you have any commitments that must go into the timetable? This might include things like regular appointments, work hours, on-going classes.
5. Write down any book titles that you would like your child to read or have read to him in the next month. Choose a couple of chapter books if you have over 7-year-olds, and half a dozen favourite picture story books for younger children. If you haven't got any book titles ready yet, you can look here for some of my own personal favourites: http://homeschoolfamilylife.com/book-shelf/books-for-children/
6. Do you have any hobbies or passions which are an important part of your week and you need to allocate time for these interests?
7. What's your refreshment? What do you like to have in your cup? Is it tea? Coffee? Herb tea? Gin? (just joking) Write down what you usually drink as refreshment during the day.

> *'The secret of all victory lies in the organisation of the non-obvious.'*
>
> MARCUS AURELIUS

PUT YOUR *EIGHT WEEK TIMETABLE* TOGETHER

Now that you have got answers to these questions, you are ready to make your *Eight Week Timetable*.

- **First decide** if you are a morning person and family or an afternoon person and family. Do you find that you and your children are more productive and ready to do sitting-down, brain work in the morning or the afternoon?
- **Then print** a single copy of the appropriate timetable on the last two pages of this chapter. There are two timetables there: one for morning people, and one for afternoon people.
- **Now fill** in the timetable.
  - Fill in your time for getting up each day.
  - Make a realistic assessment of how long it will take you to finish breakfast and complete your morning

chores. Be generous in your estimation, remembering that children always work slower than adults. Then add twenty minutes. That will give you your starting time for morning activities.
- Write down the time for starting your morning activities on your timetable.
- Add to your timetable any regular commitments or appointments that you have each week.
- Write your book titles in the box at the foot of the timetable page.
- Make your morning tea and afternoon breaks 30 minutes long. You will need this long to have a comfort break, make your drink, take ten minutes of head space, and prepare yourself for what you want to do next.

> *'Goals are dreams we convert to plans and take action to fulfil.'*
>
> ZIG ZIGLAR

- **Now add** some academics. This is going to be a very simple, easy start, so there's no need to panic.
  - The first thing we will always include on any academic timetable is the literacy component. This will go in your 'Session One' box. I have always called it 'Literacy Hour'. No matter what age your child or children are, you will have a 'Literacy Hour'. I'll deal with this in detail later in this chapter.
  - The second thing we will add to the timetable is the mathematics component which will go into the 'Session Two' box on your timetable. I will deal with this 'Numeracy Hour' in detail in the next chapter. But for now, add 'maths' to your timetable.
  - We won't add anything else to the timetable at this stage. The rest of the space in the timetable is for incidental learning, playing, reading, and doing nice things together.

> *'This one step - choosing a goal and sticking to it - changes everything.'*
>
> SCOTT REED

LITERACY HOUR

Literacy Hour is the name I have given to the time you have set aside each day for your children to improve on their literacy. It isn't necessarily an hour long, though. The length of the Literacy Hour will depend on the age of the child. Younger children will have a shorter time. Whether they are learning the alphabet or reading *Les Misérables*, whether they are learning how to hold a pencil or writing essays, for the next eight weeks, during Literacy Hour, you are just going to do two simple things with the children each day.

1. The children will have some time sitting at the table, writing.
2. The children will read and/or be read to.

If your children are young, you won't spend an hour doing this. Ten minutes for a six-year-old is plenty long enough for writing. And for a six-year-old, you may sandwich the writing/drawing time with a story before and after the pencil work.

After that, you might let the children spend a few minutes doing puzzles, or you can read poems, tell nursery rhymes, sing songs. These are excellent optionals to be included as you can manage after you have done the reading and writing.

> 'First comes thought; then organisation of that thought into ideas and plans; then transformation of those plans into reality. The beginning, as you will observe, is in your imagination.'
>
> NAPOLEON HILL

WHY DO THIS?

Reading and writing every day will ensure five good things:

1. The children will make progress in their literacy over the next few weeks.
2. You won't be overwhelmed and worried about what the children are not doing because they will be doing something.
3. You will have time to learn with me about what you can do with the children.
4. You will have time to make decisions about what you do want to teach in literacy.
5. You will make better choices without the pressure to produce something 'today'.

Over the next few weeks, you might get distracted or be tempted to panic and run off and buy something before being certain it's suitable. If that happens, remember that *you do have a plan*, and *your children are learning* and making progress.

Please don't buy yet. Instead, you can make a list of 'candidates' that you might buy later. Make your 'candidates list' in your notebook.

WRITING TIME

For each child get an exercise book. No matter how old the child, each child will need a book to write and draw in.

This is how it could look, from preschool-age, up to teenage years.

PRESCHOOL

Children will just draw a picture. You will date the picture and possibly add a short explanation label or sentence.

BEGINNING READER

Children will draw a picture and you will add a label and short sentence in large clear writing. Then read the writing to your child, follow the words with your finger and help your child to understand the connection between writing and reading.

EMERGENT READER

This child is just starting to read. He will draw a picture. Then he will dictate a short sentence and you will write the sentence in dots for him to write over your words.

EARLY READER

He will draw a picture. You will write a sentence in large clear printing. He will copy your sentence underneath.

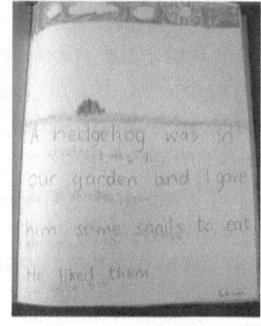

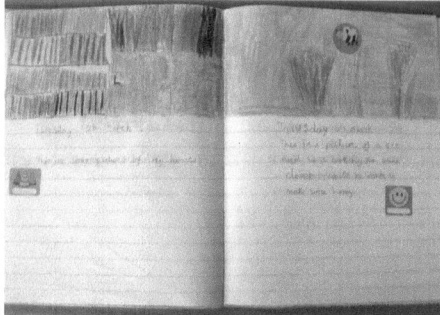

FREE READER

He will draw a picture and write a short sentence. You will help him with words.

COMPETENT READER

He will write a few sentences and illustrate his work. He can write about anything at all. You can model behaviour to him by also sitting next to him and writing in your own book.

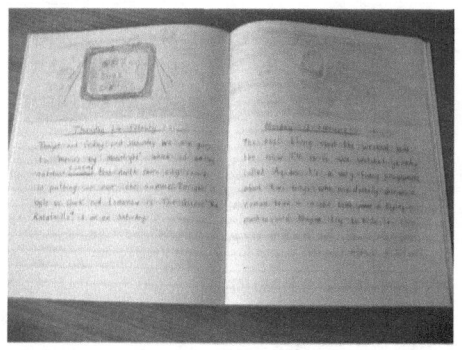

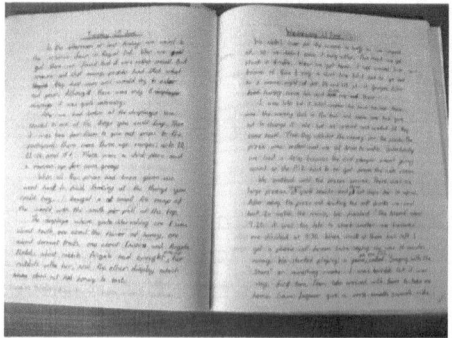

OLDER READER

He will write a page or two. He can choose his own subject. He may like to illustrate his work. You will write alongside him and give any guidance requested. You can read his work when it's complete and tick it with a pencil. If there are spelling mistakes, just write the correct spelling next to the word, use a pencil, as this is gentler and more respectful than a pen.

SIT TOGETHER

In all these cases, the children will be sitting together with you at the table, all writing, all quiet. If you like, you can put some quiet music on to help keep the atmosphere of peace and quiet work time.

The children will finish at different times and are allowed to leave the table and go and read or look at picture books or play quiet reading games until the end of Literacy Hour. The writing component of Literacy Hour will vary according to age. If you expect about 15 minutes for younger children, and about 30 minutes for the older children, you will be close to what they can manage. So most times, it won't be an hour at all.

Later on, you may decide to add grammar or spelling. But that will come later. For this to succeed, you need to set in place the good habit of sitting down to write each day at a set time.

> *'Our goals can only be reached through a vehicle of a plan, in which we must fervently believe, and upon which we must vigorously act. There is no other route to success.'*
>
> STEPHEN A. BRENNAN

It's important, when you are working with the children that you stay with them when they are working. Don't be tempted to go and sort laundry or check emails. As long as you are there, providing the atmosphere and equipment, exercising self-control, and demonstrating good work habits, you are almost certain of success.

COMPLETE YOUR TIMETABLE

- You should now have a filled in **timetable**. It should contain:
    - ✓ A sensible time for getting up and doing daily household chores.
    - ✓ All your out-of-home commitments and appointments for the next eight weeks.
    - ✓ Books that you will be reading with your children.
    - ✓ Literacy and numeracy components.
    - ✓ It also has breathing space for you to take a break

- **Display** your calendar where everyone in the family can see it. A lot of people find the fridge or a kitchen cupboard door is a good place.
- **Discuss** the calendar with the children. Talk them through it, be upbeat and positive about it. Tell them that you will be starting tomorrow morning. Give them a strong sense of things are calm and in control. You are peaceful and happy about what is going to happen tomorrow morning and it's going to be fun.
- **Now take a breath** and give yourself a little breather. Go and make a yummy dinner, or read a story to the children, or fold laundry or whatever you need to do. But don't think about the timetable again until tomorrow morning.

SUMMARY

Congratulations on completing this chapter. It has been detailed, with a lot of precise instructions on how to start off homeschooling.

This chapter is intentionally an 'overview' lesson. I've arranged it this way so that if you are brand new to homeschooling you can get started straight away. And if you are making a fresh start you will be able to do just that—make a fresh start.

> 'Always bear in mind that your own resolution to succeed is more important than any other.'
>
> ABRAHAM LINCOLN

Today, I have taken you, step by step, through making a timetable which WILL WORK if you follow it.

During the next few chapters I will:

- Continue to give you baby-steps for building up an effective, fireproof homeschooling style which will suit your own family's personality.
- Provide some powerful insights for experienced homeschoolers who are looking for a refreshing new start to their homeschooling.
- Recommend books for you to read which will help you determine more clearly the direction you want to go in your homeschooling. When you are very sure of what you where you want to go you will find it easier to 'plan

the route'.

Your homeschool timetable will be light for now, and that's intentional too. We want to get a habit of success in place and it will be so much easier to succeed with a simple timetable to work to.

And remember, we WILL be going deeper and will cover everything in great detail over the next few chapters.

ASSIGNMENT

This chapter's assignment is straightforward.

- Set aside time for yourself each week for the next little while to read, learn and think about some of the ideas we are going to be considering together.
- Print your *Eight Week Timetable* (web address on the following two pages) and fill it in.
- Display your timetable in a prominent place in your home.
- Get your children on board by discussing and explaining what is going on and what they can expect to happen.
- Start homeschooling!

OUR FAMILY'S HOMESCHOOL TIMETABLE

We Like Working in the Mornings   **Date:**

	Monday	Tuesday	Wednesday	Thursday	Friday
Early morning jobs					
Morning session one					
Morning tea					
Morning session two					
Lunch and reading time					
Afternoon activities					
Pre-dinner jobs					
Dinner					
Evening activities, story times, bedtimes					
Grown-ups' time					

This month we are reading:

www.successfulhomeschoolingmadeeasy.com/download/am-timetable

OUR FAMILY'S HOMESCHOOL TIMETABLE

We Like Working in the Afternoons   **Date:**

	Monday	Tuesday	Wednesday	Thursday	Friday
Early morning jobs					
Morning activities					
Lunch and reading time					
Afternoon session one					
Afternoon break					
Afternoon session two					
Pre-dinner jobs					
Dinner					
Evening activities, story times, bedtimes					
Grown-ups' time					

This month we are reading:

CHAPTER 3
MATHEMATICS MADE EASY

Before we start, have you got your new timetable on your fridge or cupboard or notice board? I hope it's helping you to feel calm and organised. And if you are feeling like you have cheated or something because it's all so easy—don't worry. You *haven't* cheated; you *are* homeschooling, and in this chapter you are going to add something else into your timetable.

I have a word of caution for you: RESIST all temptation to let the timetable slide. Even though your timetable is very simple, it's still important to keep to it each day. You are setting in place a good habit, and you will be glad in the long run, when you can look back and see how far you have come.

Today I am going to go through some maths ideas with you. I'll help you to see how it's not too hard at all and it's not scary. And then you can add Numeracy Hour to your timetable. Like Literacy Hour, this time won't necessarily be an hour long.

A QUESTION

How often do you meet a homeschooling mother who says, 'I really enjoy teaching maths'?

It's not very often, is it?

Of all the basic subjects, maths is probably the one that worries parents most; and many of us feel incompetent and unsure about it.

So, what do people do?

Something that happens a lot is a mother chooses a textbook or a series of textbooks, then ploughs through the book, occasionally missing out any pages that look superfluous or more trouble than they are worth; these are usually the practical pages.

She hopes her child will learn all he needs to know from the textbooks. And she breathes a little sigh of relief each day when the maths has been 'done'.

She doesn't enjoy the teaching; she doesn't see it as an enjoyable learning experience. Why? Why not?

> *'I never did well in maths – I could never seem to persuade the teacher that I hadn't meant my answers literally'*
>
> CALVIN TRILLIN

WHY IS IT NOT FUN?

I think the reasons many parents think that maths is hard is *because they weren't taught very well themselves.*

Maybe they didn't have good teachers themselves and didn't fully understand what was going on.

Maybe the teacher went too fast. Or maybe the student missed a vital step in a series of lessons, so that everything after that point didn't make much sense.

Or maybe it's just that they have forgotten so much that the textbook they have for their child looks frighteningly complicated.

> *'If you think dogs can't count, try putting three dog biscuits in your pocket and then giving Fido only two of them.'*
>
> PHIL PASTORET

But maths can be fun to teach. And fun to learn too. You don't need to be a maths whiz or have all the answers to enjoy maths.

And if you weren't good at maths or have forgotten much of the school maths that you did learn, don't worry. I will show you how you can deal with that in a positive way. I will show you how to *work alongside* your children, investigating, co-operating, discussing, and arriving at solutions together.

It's not too complicated, especially when we break it down into bite-sized pieces that we can tackle, and work step by step through the maths.

Here's the first step.

FIRST, TAKE CARE OF YOURSELF

Remember how when you are in a plane, you are told that, in an emergency, you must get your own oxygen mask on first and then take care of the children? Well it's the same with maths. First look after yourself. So get a suitable book that will make you feel totally comfortable and secure in what you are doing with the children. Remember that you are not 'stupid' or 'bad at maths'; you have either not been taught very well, or you have forgotten a lot of it.

A SIMPLE WAY TO LOOK GOOD AT MATHS

I was surprised when I discovered how many schoolteachers are also scared of teaching maths. So if you are bit worried about it, you are not alone, and you are not unusual.

A book that I liked was written for schoolteachers who are scared of teaching maths, and it's perfect for parents who want to learn some background information and prepare themselves for teaching their children maths. *Mathematics Explained for Primary Teachers* by Derek Haylock.

The book covers the full spectrum of teaching mathematics to children aged 4—11 years old. It is very reassuring and supportive, with practical teaching for the teacher, details of what you need to teach the child, and how to teach the subject. There is even a self-assessment section for you to work out what you know and what you need to learn more about.

It's a wise move to get yourself a comprehensive teacher's manual like this because:
- It is a good investment of your money.
- It will guide you through parts you are unsure of.
- It will give you confidence in teaching maths.
- It will help you to be reassured that you haven't 'missed anything'.

BE BOLD ABOUT TEACHING MATHS TO TEENS

With teens I highly recommend having a maths curriculum. If you feel like you are getting out of your depth and so is your child, then you may want to call in a tutor. Your job, at this stage, is to be a facilitator and support person for your young adult. You are the cheer leader, encouraging and searching out the opportunities for your child. You are the one with experience in researching what you need. For myself, I found a series of high school maths books that suited me and my children. When the exam system changed, I carried on using the high school maths books because we weren't going to be doing exams anyway, and I knew that I was giving my teens an excellent maths education.

When one of them wanted to go on further, I found an

Australian online high school maths programme that suited her very well. Basically, I looked at the child and assessed her needs, and then I searched for the solution. This is much better than looking for what you think is the best programme or asking someone else what they use with their child, and then trying to shoehorn your child into the programme.

> *'How many times can you subtract 7 from 83, and what is left afterwards? You can subtract it as many times as you want, and it leaves 76 every time.'*

THREE ESSENTIALS IN MATHS DEVELOPMENT

Mathematics development is at its best when it follows a similar pattern to language:
1. First there is the practical experience.
2. Then you talk about it.
3. Then you write about it.

With younger children it might be sorting, classifying, and counting. So, you will look for everyday situations where:
1. You see your child discovering things.
2. You talk about it.
3. Then you need to help him record it by drawing or writing.

It happens in a natural, almost un-noticed way.

And this theory follows through as children get older. You can keep offering your child the opportunity to handle maths equipment and discuss with your child what he is discovering before he actually writes about it.

For example:
- In studying square numbers, a child who has had lots of opportunity to play with pegs in a little peg board may notice that the number of pegs needed to fill in a square with nine pegs on each side is 81.
- For a square of only five pegs a side it's 25.
- For a square with eight pegs on each side you need 64 pegs.
- And so on.

These are the *square numbers*. When you and your child discover this together there's a thrill of pleasure and then you know that you are enjoying maths.

Using practical equipment and manipulatives to teach and practise maths concepts helps to create a strong, firm foundation of understanding. I have found this in my own experience as a homeschooling mother and as a teacher in school. Even intermediate and high school aged students can benefit from using practical equipment at times.

A Warning: Sometimes, you might think that spending time working practically is too slow and time consuming. You might wonder if you'll ever get through all your maths work. You might be tempted to leave the practical stuff and cut straight through to filling in a workbook.

DON'T. In the long run, you will actually get through more maths by spending more time on the practical, and less time on book work. And your child's understanding of maths will be very clear.

Look at the practical, hands-on work as investment time.

11 QUESTIONS TO ASK WHEN CHOOSING MATHS CURRICULUM

You don't have to use a maths curriculum to teach maths, but it makes things easier, and many people decide to buy a curriculum for maths even when they are making their own curriculum for all other subjects. This certainly makes it easier for you, as the homeschooling teacher.

I won't recommend one curriculum over others. There are lots of good choices; there is not a perfect, one-size-fits-all curriculum. It depends on you, your child; personal preferences, what's available and what you already have on your shelf.

So let me give you some pointers to choosing a good curriculum.

1. Are you looking at this a curriculum because a lot of people are using it? (Not a good reason to choose it.)

2. Does this curriculum suit you and your child? (A good reason to choose it.)
3. Are the pages too cluttered or too plain?
4. Do you understand the concepts yourself?
5. Do you think those concepts are well explained?
6. Does the book come with a comprehensive teacher's manual?
7. Do you think you need one? (If you need an answer sheet you probably need a teacher's manual.)
8. Does the book you've chosen teach the correct types of weights and measures for your country?
9. Have you been able to get a copy of the book to look at carefully at your leisure?
10. Have you asked others using the curriculum what they like or dislike about it?
11. Have you given yourself plenty of time alone to look through the maths book?

HOW TO HAVE YOUR CHILDREN BEGGING YOU FOR MORE MATHS

When your children are asking for maths and choosing it, you know you are doing well. It won't happen to us all, but we can do things to increase the possibility of children asking for maths and even calling 'mathematics' their favourite 'subject'.

Even if you have a fabulous curriculum, it will still have limitations. So you can look for ways of supplementing your curriculum with other maths activities.

For example, other activities could include things like:
- Snap and dominoes are helpful for younger children.
- Homemade maths games.
- Maths board games.
- Times table books and CDs help with rote learning.
- You and your children can invent your own games.
- A very limited amount of computer maths games or even no computer games for younger children. The computer games always look better than they are and that they are worth. And I have seen children avoid the learning part and cheat the programme to play the games.
- There a lots of lovely picture books that teach maths concepts. For example, the *Sir Cumference* book series.

COOKING AND SHOPPING

Cooking and shopping are great ways of practising maths skills and having fun at the same time.

A trip to the supermarket includes dozens of maths activities; older children could do mental calculations of how much you have spent as you walk round or calculate which of two brands of a product works out cheaper.

And **estimating** is one of the most common and useful daily maths applications you can develop in your child.

CHECK OUT THE LIBRARY

You might like to get maths books from the library. This is my favourite way to teach maths; it's so easy and makes maths such good fun. The call number is 519—520 for children's books and you can look under call number 371 in the adult section for teaching ideas. Also, you can collect a few maths games books for your bookshelf.

DON'T FORGET TO ENJOY MATHS

If you are still feeling unsure about enjoying maths:
- Find another homeschooling family who is enjoying maths; ask them for tips and suggestions.
- Set up a Games Afternoon and invite friends round.
- Make Fridays (or a day that suits) your maths games day.

You will soon notice the improvement in attitude to maths in yourself and your children.

> *'The essence of mathematics is not to make simple things complicated, but to make complicated things simple.'*
> S. GUDDER

SUMMARY

In this chapter you have been shown five components of making the teaching of mathematics easy and fun. To summarise, they are:
1. First look after yourself.
2. Three essentials in maths development.
3. Eleven Questions to ask when choosing curriculum.
4. How to have your children begging you for more maths.
5. Don't forget to enjoy maths.

ASSIGNMENT

1. Consider curriculum.
   - If you already have a curriculum, check out the list in this chapter and see how it measures up. If you are happy with the curriculum, it should measure up pretty well.
   - If you are considering a curriculum, use the questions to help you decide.
   - If you are not yet ready for curriculum, use the ideas in this chapter to enjoy informal maths. Especially look for opportunities to practise mathematics informally. And get books from the library with ideas and games each week.
2. Make a list of all the fun activities you can do with your children for maths.
3. Next time you visit the library make sure you get a few maths books. If you find the books really useful, consider buying one or two for your bookshelf.
4. Add 'Numeracy Hour' to your timetable.
   - Tell your children that this week you will also be including maths in your daily timetable.
   - Make it fun, have some sort of game in Numeracy Hour.
   - Prepare ahead of time, so that lesson time is fun and easy.
   - As with Literacy, you won't be spending an hour writing. The children will be mainly doing activities and playing games. Older children will spend about 30 minutes writing. And you will also want to allow time for things like discussion, experimenting and thinking.
   - If you want a little bit more on maths games, you will find more games ideas here: www.successfulhomeschoolingmadeeasy.com/download/ideas-4-maths

CHAPTER 4
WELCOME HOME!

WHAT TO EXPECT WHEN YOU START HOMESCHOOLING YOUR SCHOOL CHILD

Although a lot of people start homeschooling their children as soon as the child reaches school age, there are many children who have spent time in school before they start being homeschooled.

If a child has been to school before, it will be different. The children respond to homeschooling in a variety of different ways, and it takes time to settle into homeschooling.

If you have just brought your child out of school or if you are planning to do so, the best person to talk to is someone else who has walked this path before you. And here are some women who have done just that: I have asked mothers of schooled children to give their tips and experiences.

If you are homeschooling from the beginning, don't skip this chapter—I am sure you will be encouraged by these words or encouragement and wisdom from homeschoolers.

I know you'll be inspired by their stories and wisdom. They are homeschooling mums from all over the world. You'll see that their experiences are all different, but their pleasure in homeschooling is the same. (names have been changed.)

Anna

It is one thing to homeschool your children from the beginning, but I assure you it is completely different when you take them out of school. Here is a brief synopsis of our mistakes and what we have learnt when we took all four of our children out of school.

The first six months of homeschooling was an emotional roller coaster, and one of the most important things I have learnt and so wished I had done (been advised of) is the importance of de-schooling your child. No matter how it looks, they will not fall behind by doing this. I vaguely remember one person advising me and I automatically shrugged off the idea because I thought the children would fall behind—I now know better

Other classic mistakes we made:
1. Bringing school home and treating home like school.
2. Overwhelming the children with the amount of work (At the time I thought 100-200 easy sums a day was reasonable) It was not until we sat down with them and they talked through a normal day at school that we realised they were only used to five sums a day—Whoops!
3. Not advising the children that work will be marked—the children were not used to their work being marked, and on some occasions put down any old thing.
4. Not informing the children of our standards i.e. If it is wrong then yes, we do it again until it is correct (For some reason my children had learnt at school that you had to do your work, not that it has to be correct)
5. Setting time slots for work, this became a big no-no for us—at school they had learnt how to waste time during their time slots, therefore for us a more effective way was to do a certain number of pages i.e. two pages maths, one page grammar, etc.

My children are normal children who had gone to a highly rated primary school in our area and according to reports, were doing well, and at their age-level—we have learnt so much from our homeschooling experience already and realised how many of what we considered fundamentals the children had not been taught at school and how fortunate we were to be homeschooling

Beatrice

My two older children were in school for a few years and when we started homeschooling we were encouraged to leave academics for at least six months and just spend time reading together and playing games and just enjoying each other's company. Basically a de-schooling time. We did this and it was really beneficial. It can seem really hard at first as the children are so used to being in a structured environment and they have the 'school mindset' that we should be writing, filling in workbooks etc. I must admit this has been a challenge for me as well as the children. I used to be a 'Mother Help' in the children's classrooms and so it is very easy to try and duplicate this environment at home.

My advice would be just relax and enjoy each other. Read heaps of wonderful books together, play lots of games. We learnt heaps about world history and geography and local history and geography through these games as well as spending enjoyable family time together.

I would also suggest spending time enjoying local parks and walks, spend time baking, crafting etc. Maybe go on a trip together enjoying and exploring local history, geography, and wildlife etc.

I really think the biggest obstacle is our mindsets. Especially if we have gone through the school system (which most of us have). So we need to really work on this and think about what it is we are really wanting for our children and how will we achieve this. If I had my time over again I would relax more, enjoy them more, spend heaps of time doing things with them and create as many warm, fun and memorable memories as I could.

Catherine

My biggest surprise when I brought my children out of school was my own fear of 'not doing enough'. School is product focused. We know what we learnt at school because we have this piece of paper and questions I answered. I did not believe this showed learning and yet I battled with knowing we were learning even if we didn't 'fill in the blanks' today. I discovered that our conversations showed we had connected with things.

If you are taking a child out of school, I would recommend that you
1. Take plenty of time to reconnect with your child. It will take much longer than you think, and each child is different in this regard—some will only need a few weeks, others will need a year.
2. Read aloud together (any age child), go for lovely walks and observe things—enjoy being together and getting to know each other. Ask questions about what they like, and you share likewise.

3. Spend time getting a clear idea of what you want to do in your home education. It will be different to other families—no two home educators do it the same and that is fine.
4. Don't try to launch into a full day of study—slowly add one thing at a time until it is second nature, and then add in the next thing.
5. Be prepared for hard days and on those days be kind to yourself and your children and find something nice to do (maybe a special morning tea). Don't beat yourself up about it. It is a big change in lifestyle for everyone.
6. Find some things which your children are interested in and read and talk about those things; this will help them to develop their interest and re-ignite their love for learning. They might be very used to being told what to learn and when.
7. Find some encouraging books or blogs about home education and become well informed about your new job. You don't have to agree with everything you read. It is a great thing to talk to your children about what you are learning. This is a wonderful example to them that we never stop learning and that adults sometimes struggle to learn new things, and the joy of accomplishing it.
8. Take some time for yourself. Be sure to nurture yourself. Organise to have a quiet moment in the day where you can gather your thoughts and refresh yourself—the children need this too.
9. Journal about the days that go well so you can read about them again and see if there are particular things over time which work well for your family.

Diana

Spend some time just enjoying being together and finding out what works. Don't be afraid to ditch something that does not work.

Eleanor

My child wasn't happy at school. He couldn't understand why children had to leave their parents for so long and spend the day at the school with other people who he did not know or particularly like or have anything in common with. He felt like he spent the days in fear and anxiety. He told me, 'I just want to be at home with you Mummy. I learn more at home mummy.' (He was only six.)

When I started homeschooling I was surprised at how much I loved it. I thought I would struggle but it became a lifestyle, not school at home. It felt like we got our identity and strength as a family back.

I now have happy, content, intelligent, and more independent children. The home influences are more wholesome, and we can teach our children about our faith without fear of them being made to feel weird. Our son's confidence went from wanting to die and not wanting to exist, to a child with a healthy glow and happy heart. For my family it has been an answer to prayer.

I can't think of any disadvantages to homeschooling compared to school. It is not hard like you think it's going to be. Your relationship with your family seems to take on a whole new level of awareness, connection, closeness, and commitment. Our children have the happy lives I envisioned when they were babies. You cannot compare home educating life to school; they are so different, and school cannot give our children anything near to what our lifestyle can. Parents are the biggest influences in a child's life. Whatever made me think that sending him away to school every day was going to help him turn out happy, confident and successful?

Fiona

When we started homeschooling I was surprised at how quickly I burned out. I was trying to do too much, and it wasn't as fun for the children.

I would say, do not try to recreate school at home. Have fun for a while, relax, whatever you do will be better than anything they would have done in school. You don't have to cram a ton of stuff in. Give them a reason to love it. Let them pursue their passions. Trust your instincts.

Gina

My advice would be DO IT! It will be the best thing you have ever done. Don't expect to reproduce a classroom environment at home. Be realistic with goals and timetables. Spend the first few months getting into spending joyful time with your child. Read, go on outings, cuddle in bed in the morning, go for walks, have fun, play games, cook. The days will fly by and your relationship with your child will improve so much that the work will naturally follow.

HARRIET

My son was six when I started homeschooling, I was blown away by how natural it was. I had helped him to sit, crawl, walk and talk, we had shared all normal learning moments, homeschooling was a natural extension of that.

I love being around my children, always wanted to home school, would of right the way through, for all my six children, had I not been ill. Wonderful memory-making years, loving, laughing, learning, living together. Not always easy, but much better than rushed mornings getting everyone out the door to school, then losing the best hours of the day, only to have them return, mad rush of homework, tea, bath time...then bed, with a story and a quick prayer.

My advice to someone planning to bring their child out of school—DO IT, no seriously, it's very rewarding, time consuming.... make sure you:
1. Get some time for you.
2. Make time for you and your significant other, if you have one, to have some adult alone time.
3. If you have more than one child, make a date with each child, take turns with your partner if you have one, get inside your child's head, know them, listen to them, laugh, cry, and share with them.
4. Household tasks, duties and chores are part of life and learning, include them as part of your schooling and part of your school day.

ISABELLE

I was convinced to homeschool when I observed the class and saw how the teacher spent time teaching the slow learners while leaving the other children to do worksheets. So much time was wasted in classroom management and waiting for everyone to toe the line that the actual hours of learning time seemed quite spare.

My biggest surprise when I started homeschooling was how

close my daughter and I became, and how many opportunities there were to learn things that were way beyond grade level for my child. I was also astounded at the staggering number of resources and websites that cater for learners at home, from primary all the way to college level.

I like the freedom we had to explore various opportunities like travel during the school year. Homeschooling is portable. The whole world is your classroom. Homeschooling cultivates an enquiring mind and gives a child the opportunity to develop her gifting and skills and allow her interests to drive her to learn more things in-depth. Homeschooling also allows a parent to bond more deeply with their child and impart to them values that are important to the family.

My advice to people thinking of homeschooling would be first, the homeschooling mum should 'detox' from the idea that homeschooling is equivalent to school at home. She should be very clear about WHY she wants to homeschool because that will carry her through the tough times. The first few months after a child is out of school could be spent doing enjoyable things like field trips, read-alouds, etc. These activities will, hopefully, re-kindle the child's original love for learning and discovering their world. The parent should do a lot of research regarding how to approach her homeschooling—which methods and resources will be most appealing and useful for her child's learning style and interests. I think there's value in the parent and child discussing what their homeschool will look like, what activities they'll do, and how much time will be spent doing studies or service or work, etc. A parent will find having a clear educational philosophy is invaluable, i.e. She could clarify for herself what education means. Is it the dumping of information and knowledge in a child's mind to be regurgitated later in the form of a test? Does education equal exploring and discovering the world for themselves? What does it mean to be well-educated?

> 'The task of the modern educator is not to cut down jungles, but to irrigate deserts.'
>
> C. S. Lewis

I would also encourage a new homeschooling parent to join a homeschooling association or learning co-op for encouragement, shared activities, and networking.

Jenny

I was surprised at how easy it was to be so busy that we were hardly at home when we started homeschooling. By that I mean that it's easy to enrol in classes and extracurricular activities and go to everything the homeschool group organises, so you don't feel like you are doing nothing, and then wonder why you are so exhausted.

I like having the time to build a relationship with my daughter again and having time for her to learn at her own pace, and the freedom to make our own timetable.

My advice would be to do it with confidence that you are doing the right thing for your family. We decided that it didn't matter what others thought as our child's happiness and education were our main priority. Plus I think it was a bonus that she is our fourth, so we weren't as easily swayed as if she were our first child. (Experience is a blessing.)

Kate

My biggest surprise when I started homeschooling was the public ignorance and opposition. The public forcing their uninvited opinions thoughtlessly and implying I am a bad or foolish parent. To be honest I do not wish to defend home education to everyone, I just want to get on with it.

My daughter is a lot more secure and confident around other people and children now. Her health is much better from walking and eating much more healthily than at school.

Lucy

The biggest surprise to me when I started homeschooling was how easy it was. I can tailor my learning programme to each individual child's learning needs and interests. We can really get to know each other well as a family.

The hard part is the constancy of children with me ALL the time with no breaks. The challenge to schedule in housekeeping type activities.

My advice would be—go for it. There are so many benefits that will be slowly revealed to you as you proceed along the journey. You will all learn so much. Ask lots of people about their experiences and then choose a path that best suits your family. Write down your reasons for homeschooling at the outset, because when challenges come (and they will) you have got something to hang on to. Don't give up easily; there are answers to all your challenges somewhere- just keep looking. This is a life experience like no other, enjoy it. There will be plenty of naysayers—get over it. Eventually even some of them may be converted as they see it working so well, and it will. Remember this is a long-term project.

Moira

I would advise—Do it. It is easier to deal with problems than to pick up the pieces of your child's emotions and psyche for the rest of their lives due to problems encountered at school and the personalities they have formed there by influence of teachers and other students.

Nancy

I was surprised at how quickly I 'got my daughter back'. She became chatty, relaxed, responsive, and happy again. Also, that it wasn't anywhere near as hard as I had feared.

I like the flexibility of homeschooling. This is not merely in being able to alter my teaching approach to suit her learning style, but also in subjects studied and individualising the programme and also in lifestyle. Wonderful!

The disadvantages are just selfish personal sacrifices. Those being mainly in time alone, my own career progression (I gave up work to home educate) and of course, less money. Wouldn't trade any of them for what we now have though.

My advice is that you only have this time and opportunity to be with your child, and truly meet their needs, once. It is precious. Set aside the fears of 'I wouldn't be able to do it, I don't have the patience or ability, and how can I match what they do at school'. They are all false fears and I am living proof of it. Of course you can do it. You don't have to be a saint. Don't even try to match what they do at school—you really wouldn't like it. In fact, write down how many hours of 'real' teaching time they have at school (not homework) and you will see the truth. You achieve far more at home. It is tailored to your child, rather than the masses and will engage them more.

Yes, there will be hard times when you butt heads, but you already do that now (usually over homework). There is a ton of support, help and advice out there. Make every use of it but try not to be overwhelmed by potential information overload. It is easy to feel inadequate in the early days or at low times. Stay true to your heart and your child and be led by those, not by what every else is doing. What suits them will possibly not suit you. You may even find they are not achieving quite what you think they are and have fears and issues of their own, so take time to chat. Find a friend or mentor. Whatever you do, do not rush out in a flight of panic and buy, buy, buy. Take your time and get wise to what is available and what will suit your and your child. One person's curriculum could be your nightmare or revelation. Again, take your time. Finally—take the bull by the horns and give it a go. You will be amazed, relieved and thankful.

Olivia

I was surprised at how easy it is, once you find what works and what does not work for your children.

I have more confidence in my children, and they have an ability to wisely choose their own areas of interest and know how to find the answers to questions etc. Their research skills and desire to learn are much improved.

There are not really any disadvantages to homeschooling but we are finding it hard to put up with the rubbish we get from friends and especially family who know nothing at all about home education but seem to think my children are better to go to school. Peer pressure on the parents is the hard part but the children seem to find their friends would rather be home schooled too. The only disadvantage we find is that we are 'different'. And maybe that my children have to wait until late afternoon and weekends to play with their friends.

I think the hardest part especially when you're starting out is other people and their opinions about it when they mostly know very little, also the lack of support for home educating families, although it's becoming more widely accepted.

Penelope

Talk with other homeschooling parents online and in your community to help answer some of your questions and make you more at ease as you get started. Don't spend a bunch of money on curriculum until you have an idea of your child's learning style and what works for him or her, and for you, too.

SUMMARY

It's Stephanie here again. What can I say? These ladies offer so much reassurance and enthusiasm. And you can see how they love being with their children. Listen to them and be encouraged.

ASSIGNMENT

Take time to read carefully through this chapter. There's a lot to read, and it is relevant to you and your situation as a homeschooler or potential homeschooler. Be encouraged to ENJOY this wonderful lifestyle.

CHAPTER 5
FIREPROOF YOUR HOMESCHOOL

Are you keeping to your simple timetable?

This is the most important thing you can do.

When you keep to your timetable, you will find it easier to live your homeschool life in a calm, orderly way, without exhausting yourself or your children. And if you are reading a recommended chapter a week from this book, then you will have had two or three weeks of successful homeschooling already.

In this chapter, we will add something to the timetable, and then move focus on to other things. But we are not getting off-track at all. In fact, you'll see in the long run, that we are actually still on track and going in the right direction.

> *'Don't wait until everything is just right. It will never be perfect. There will always be challenges, obstacles and less than perfect conditions. So what? Get started now. With each step you take, you will grow stronger and stronger, more and more skilled, more and more self-confident, and more and more successful.'*
>
> MARK VICTOR HANSEN

YOUR TIMETABLE

If you are following your timetable each day, you should be feeling pretty confident about homeschooling by now. You are getting up at a time that suits your family, you are completing your early morning activities in a timely manner, and each day, you are doing some sort of 'seat work' with your children. Everything is low-key and looking like the sort of thing that suits your own special family. It won't look like any other family, and it should not be too stressful.

ARE THINGS GOING SMOOTHLY?

If things are not going too smoothly, don't panic.

You may need to adjust some of the times slightly to make

> *If at first you don't succeed, try to hide your astonishment.*

things run more efficiently. That would be quite reasonable at this stage.

And if this timetable is very different for you and your family, you can also expect to have had a couple of meltdowns.

Don't worry about this.

Forgive yourself. Forgive your children.

Then make a fresh start tomorrow morning. Gradually, you will notice that the meltdowns and disappointments will become less frequent, as you become more secure and settled in homeschooling.

And each time you 'fall over', just pick yourself up and start again. Eventually, you will 'fall' less often, and you will find it easier to stick to the plan.

What's already on your timetable?

Your timetable now has:
- A literacy time.
- A numeracy time.
- A sensible plan for your mornings.
- Space for breaks and meals.
- A reading aloud time.
- A space for events that you are committed to throughout the week; things like courses and appointments.

That's a pretty good start. Well done!

Add something new to the timetable

Now you will add one more small thing to your timetable.

Make a list of enjoyable things that you and your children all enjoy

Now, choose one of these fun things and slot it into your timetable somewhere.

Put what you want where you want it to be.

It's up to you. The only rule is that it has to be something nice that you all (or most of you) enjoy.

Now that you've added something to your timetable, we can start looking at the main part of this chapter. This next section is the start of a multi-part lesson on working out your homeschooling style. It's an important part of this book. Doing this well will ensure a successful homeschooling experience for you and your children.

WHAT IS 'AN EDUCATION'?

Do you know exactly what you want to do with your children? Do you have a vision for your children? Your family? Your homeschool plan?

This is the single most important thing you can ever do in your homeschooling career. And for the next few chapters I will guide you through working out your vision for your homeschool and your family, so that, when you are finished, (if you do it thoroughly and carefully, taking it seriously and giving the job the attention it deserves), you will be almost fireproof in your homeschooling. You will have notes that you can pull out at any time to encourage yourself and remind yourself of what you're doing and why you're doing it.

So work with me, commit to accepting this wonderful challenge as well as you possibly can. And we will start right now, with some questions for you to think about and answer.

WHAT TYPE OF PERSON ARE YOU?

> *'If you're going to keep your children out of schools you had better decide what an education means because no one is going to do it for you.'*
> DAVID GUTERSON *Family Matters: Why Homeschooling Makes Sense*

It is said that there are three types of person in the world; those who make things happen, those who watch things happen, and those who haven't got the foggiest idea what's happening.

In home educating circles we have plenty of the first type of person; the ones who make things happen.

It's good to know that.

It's good especially when you face opposition.

Because as a first group type you are very likely to face opposition. Possibly from:
- Neighbours
- Family
- Strangers
- Friends

Because you are different you will be questioned and watched by those around you. And even your own thoughts and doubts will attack you and leave you scared, unsure, and ready to run.

NOT EVERYONE WILL UNDERSTAND

Some people will not understand why you are choosing to home educate your children. So it's important to have it really clear in your own mind:
- What you are doing.
- Why you are doing it.
- Where you want to end up.

Then when the going gets tough, you will have resources within you that will support you and carry you through.

> *'The vision is always solid and reliable; the vision is always a fact. It is the reality that is often a fraud.'*
>
> G K CHESTERTON

WHAT? AND WHY?

When you work out your vision, you need to spend time thinking about what you want, why you want it and where you are heading.

It's a good idea to set aside time to think about the answers really carefully and write down any ideas you might have.

So stop now, make sure that you have at least twenty minutes of uninterrupted quiet time. Make sure you are comfortable, and that you have a good pen, a notebook or paper, maybe a drink. Some pleasant music. Music can be very helpful for setting the scene, calming your spirit, settling your mind so that you can think well and clearly. Choose your own favourite relaxing music. You might decide to work on your computer. Try not to use your phone unless you can type on your phone as fast as on a full-size keyboard. You need to keep it easy to do so that you can focus on how you want to answer the questions. Now it's time to work through the following two questions.

QUESTIONS

1. *'What do you want to achieve in your life?'* I am not thinking only of home educating, but your life as a whole. What do you want to achieve in your LIFE?
   - You might want to provide for yourself and your family a sense of permanence in a world of change.
   - You might want to live a simple, clutter-free lifestyle.

- You might want to become really good at your hobby or skill or sport.
- You might want to run a marathon or learn to fly a glider plane.
- You might have a desire to pass on your values to your children and help your children to become successful in the areas of life you value.
- Maybe you want to read the 100 great books.

Write down your plans and ambitions for your life. It might take several pages of writing, or it might be just a few lines of writing. But the main thing is that you do write something NOW.

2. *Why do you want to home educate your children?*
    - Maybe you are looking for a simple family lifestyle.
    - Maybe you are eager to implement a particular educational approach in your family.
    - Maybe you want to place an emphasis on academics.
    - Maybe you believe you can do a better job than school.
    - Maybe you enjoy your child's company and you want to enjoy his childhood and growing up years with him.
    - Maybe you want to homeschool out of faith conviction.

Take some time now, to write down the answers to these two questions about what you want to achieve in your own life and why you want to homeschool. Don't rush. The answers to these questions are important.

When you have the answers to these two questions in place it will be much easier for you to know WHAT you want your child to learn and HOW you will go about homeschooling your child and organising your daily life in a way that is comfortable for you and your family.

> *'Success is not the key to happiness. Happiness is the key to success. If you love what you are doing, you will be successful.'*
>
> HERMAN CAIN (American businessman, author, and speaker)

Then we can talk about curriculum, educational goals and more.

THREE RECOMMENDED BOOKS

A book that I heartily recommend to people who are working out their vision is *The Seven Habits of Highly Effective People* by Stephen Covey. This is a modern classic and is very helpful in offering practical steps to working out what you want to achieve and what is important in your life.

Other books I have found helpful when considering my vision are books which talk about how people overcame great difficulties in their lives.

Two books which jump to mind are: *Life is So Good* by George Dawson—the autobiography of a man who learned to read when he was 98.

And *One Step Beyond* which tells the story of Chris Moon who recovered from losing his right leg and arm in a landmine blast and ran the London Marathon a year after leaving hospital.

You may notice that I've not recommended a homeschooling book yet.

That's deliberate. I will recommend a couple of my favourite homeschool books later. But to begin with, it's helpful to get right back to basics and really have clear in your own mind why you are homeschooling and what you want to achieve in your own life.

SUMMARY

In this chapter I have encouraged you to add a fun activity to your timetable.

I have guided you through the first questions on working out what you want to achieve in your own life and why you want to homeschool. Considering and writing down the answers to these two questions might take some time, but it's important to getting homeschooling going really successfully.

I have recommended some books for you to read.

ASSIGNMENT

1. Add the fun activity to your timetable. Tell the children that you have this new thing to look forward to each week.
2. Work through the questions in this chapter. I urge you to do it as soon as you possibly can. You just need at least twenty minutes of peace and quiet. Maybe you could get up half an hour earlier tomorrow morning. Or maybe you could use a timeslot when you have dropped your children at a class and you are sitting in your car waiting for them.

Whatever time you choose, be creative and proactive and do it soon. You'll be so glad you did.

3. See if you can find an inspirational book to read—try one of the books I've recommended or find another book which inspires you to tackle something hard but worthwhile. This is important as you work out your vision and then follow up on achieving your vision. Reading good books (not necessarily homeschooling books) and building up your library is a great way to develop your homeschooling skills.

CHAPTER 6
THREE QUESTIONS...
EVERY SUCCESSFUL HOMESCHOOLER KNOWS THE ANSWERS TO

If you are reading a chapter of this book each week, you are now heading into your fourth week of successful homeschooling using your simple timetable. I am sure you'll agree it's not too hard, is it? Remember to keep focused on what is listed on your timetable, and try, as much as you can, to *keep to the timetable*.

At the same time as keeping to your simple timetable, you are working on getting a really clear picture of your goals and desires in homeschooling. In this chapter, I will show you how to do some more work on discovering exactly what sort of homeschooling career you want to have with and for your children.

YOUR TIMETABLE

You now have literacy, numeracy, something that's fun, and reading aloud times in your timetable. You also have lots of free time in your day. Free time is any time that isn't allocated on the timetable. Today you can add something else to the timetable. But don't worry. I'm not going to let you get too busy. The beauty of this addition is that it is fun for you to prepare and will take less than two minutes for you to put into practice.

Choose some classical music which will be played throughout the day. You can choose your favourite composer to start with. And if you have never had any connection with classical music, let me recommend Mozart. Choose something popular, light, and easy to enjoy at first listening; maybe Eine Kleine Nacht Music or a piano concerto or Symphony 40.

You might like to play this music as the morning chores are coming to an end and the children are gathering together at the dining table. Write it on your timetable as 'music appreciation'. At this stage you don't have to do anything else except hear it.

So no need for comments or discussion unless this comes up naturally.

THREE QUESTIONS

In the last chapter, you answered two important questions: what you want to do in your own life, and why you want to teach your children at home.

When you know the answers to these questions, you can build on the information, focusing on what you believe in, so that when you face opposition and discouragement, as you will, you won't listen to the naysayers.

And you will even resist listening to the little voice in your head that, on negative days, will try to criticise what you are doing.

In this chapter, you have three more questions to think about. These are questions that successful homeschoolers know the answers to. And your answers will help you focus on what's right for you and your own children.

> *'There is no doubt that it is around the family and the home that all the greatest virtues, the most dominating virtues of human society, are created, strengthened and maintained.'*
>
> WINSTON CHURCHILL

Spend time this week considering your answers to the questions. Read books around the subject. Take your time. The results, and what you will do with the results, will be worth the time spent.

So, onto the questions:

1. *What things are important for you and your child—what do you want to achieve with your child and for your child?*
    - Is it qualifications and exam results?
    - Is it books shared?
    - Is it experiences shared?
    - Is it building happy memories?
    - Is it passing on your faith and beliefs?
    - Is it having lots of friends?
    - Is it having a good relationship with family?
    - Is it getting into university?
    - What other things?

Write down your answers. Include anything that is important to you in relation to your children.

2. *Where would you like to be in your life with your child in ten years' time?*
3. *How will home educating help you to achieve your goal or dream?*

Spend time *thinking about the answers to these questions.*
Work out *what it is that's really important to your family.*
Go deeper *than the first level of answer which might be something like, 'My family is important' or 'My faith is important'.*
Consider *what's really important and name it to yourself.*
Write *it down.*
Add *to your notes over the coming days, weeks, and months.*
Use *it to refer to when you are feeling distracted from your vision or worried about whether you are doing things right.*

> 'Just don't give up trying to do what you really want to do. Where there's love and inspiration, I don't think you can go wrong.'
>
> ELLA FITZGERALD

BOOKS ON HOMESCHOOLING

Finally, I want to mention books on the topic of homeschooling. There are hundreds of them, but I have just a couple here that I would recommend for anyone. I think these will help you when you are working out your homeschooling vision are:

- *How Children Learn at Home* by Alan Thomas. This isn't an easy book to get hold of, but it's worth the effort. In this book, Alan Thomas discusses his research among home educators in Australia and Great Britain. He noticed that the more experienced homeschoolers gravitated towards an informal style of education, very different from school education, and he saw the children developing their own learning agendas. It's an ideal book to refer to and to show to sceptical family members. Do take the time to hunt it down and read it. You will find it encouraging and helpful.
- *For the Children's Sake* by Susan Schaeffer Macaulay. This is a home education classic; it gives a short introduction to the philosophy and practical application

of learning at home. The author inspires with her warmth and gentle attitude; she covers each subject with comments and thoughts. This book is the antithesis to the high pressure, exam-related, politically correct stress of school learning, and focuses on learning as a pleasurable activity which will last a lifetime. Many people would say that this is the book every home educator should start by reading and should have on their shelf. I tend to agree with them.

> *'The future depends on what we do in the present.'*
> MOHANDAS GANDHI

SUMMARY

In this chapter you have worked hard at answering three questions which will help you to focus on what you want to achieve with your children.

By answering these questions, you will clarify your own thoughts, hopes and dreams for your family and you will have a clear goal for your homeschool.

After that, I will help you to achieve your goal.

ASSIGNMENT

Your assignment today is two-fold:
1. Answer the questions in this chapter.
2. Spend some time reading about homeschooling ideas and experiences. Start with the books recommended in this chapter if you can.

CHAPTER 7
FULFIL YOUR DREAMS

What do you think is the best way to ensure happy and successful homeschooling?

It's not your academic ability. It's not your children's academic ability. It's not the attitude of your children. It's actually your attitude. Homeschooling can be absolutely wonderful or really difficult. It all depends on your attitude.

When you are feeling calm, peaceful and in control, you will have a calm, peaceful, homeschooling family.

There are more questions in this chapter, and these questions are very much focused on you and your own needs and wants. They are aimed at helping you see how well you are taking care of yourself (and so setting yourself up to succeed)., and how you can make an even better job of taking care of yourself.

> When you are feeling calm, peaceful and in control, you will have a calm, peaceful homeschooling family.

This is a crucial part of homeschooling.

So be encouraged to spend some time looking at the questions and working out good answers for yourself and your family.

TIMETABLE

I hope your music addition is going well. If you did enjoy Mozart last week, try adding another composer to your repertoire. Maybe Tchaikovsky's *Piano Concerto No 1*.

Keep following your timetable as closely as you can. If there is something on the timetable which is proving really hard to do, consider whether you want to persist with it, or if you would be better to offer some flexibility and make a change around the tricky thing.

Meanwhile, we need to add something else to the timetable. Do you have a free afternoon? An afternoon when the children have their own free time? That can now be blocked out as 'art' afternoon. Or, if you work in the afternoons, you could block out some time in the morning.

Start easily with whatever art materials you have in the house. Then, as the children ask for or appear to need materials, add them to your shopping list and get them next time you go out, or order online. Allow the children some free time with the art materials to explore, and then if you have time, and you think they need some focus, you can ask them to create something from one of the books that you have been reading to them recently.

N.B. If you don't have a free afternoon this week, *then leave this activity.*

TAKE CARE OF YOUR CHILDREN'S MOTHER

Working out the answers to questions about what you are doing and why you are doing it is a great way to keep focused in home education.

In the last chapter, I asked you to consider what you want to achieve with your family. In this chapter, there are four questions about how you take care of a very important and key person in your family. I am asking you about yourself, and how you are taking care of yourself.

Often in homeschooling, we focus very much on the children and the teaching, and in particular, the teaching of academics. This is back-to-front thinking.

We need to first take care of ourselves (if you don't take care of yourself who will? And what sort of example are you setting your daughters for when they grow up? And what are your sons learning about how to treat their wives? And what sort of message are you sending your family about how they should treat you?) Your home is a family home, not a child-focused home. It's your home too, and it must be a place of peace, refuge and refreshment for the adults of the home as well as the children.

The first question I have for you today is an important question, and it's the one, of all the questions I ask homeschooling mothers, that usually stymies them.

> To STYMIE: *to thwart, baffle, block, embarrass, hinder, obstruct.*

Mothers are often stymied when

asked what they do to take care of themselves. And when pressed, they slowly realise that they are behaving disgracefully and being quite mean and unkind to themselves.

It is not admirable to be mean to yourself. To give to others at the expense of your own well-being. It's not holy and it's not spiritual. It's foolish. If you are not in top form, feeling rested each morning, feeling confident about each day, how you can you give your best to your family, and homeschool in the way that you want? Be a wise mother and take time to care for yourself. And it's never too late to start doing this. So here are the questions:

1. *What am I doing to nurture and develop my own growth?*

If you are finding it hard to know what you are doing for yourself then maybe this is a good time to make a change. Work out what you really want to do for yourself. It doesn't need to be big, and it can certainly be done without a detrimental effect on the family. Then carve out a place in your life to do this very thing.

2. *Do I have a tendency to live vicariously?*

To live vicariously means to live through someone else—often, it is your child.

3. *What am I giving my child which is what I want or wanted as a child?*

This is quite a common phenomenon; people often give their children what they feel like they missed out on as a child.

In fact, it is often said that parents are so busy giving their children what they themselves missed out on that they forget to give their children what they DID have as a child.

For example, a man who was brought up with few material possessions, but had a father who played with him and took him to the park might work hard to give his son lots of lovely toys but not understand the value of time for playing and trips to the park with his son. This is a generalisation to help you get the picture and see what I am trying to say.

> *It is not admirable to be mean to yourself. It's not holy, and it's not spiritual. It's foolish. If you are not in top form, feeling rested each morning, feeling confident about each day, how can you give your best to your family and homeschool in the way that you want to do it? Be a wise mother and take time to care for yourself.*

NOW ASK YOURSELF:

- What can I do about vicarious living?
- What am I really trying to give my children?
- Why?

Did you want tennis lessons as a child? Join a tennis club and get some tuition.

Did you want music lessons as a child? Take lessons now for yourself.

Did you always want to be an artist? Go to art lessons yourself. Buy yourself some beautiful art supplies and set aside time to enjoy them.

Does YOUR CHILD want ballet lessons? Then see which ballet school will suit your child and your budget.

Give your child what suits him or her, and not what you wish you had. Then find out ways to fulfil your own achievements and dreams.

FULFIL YOUR OWN DREAMS

Fulfilling your own dreams need not cost the earth; if you are creative and determined, you will find a way.

I know someone who always wanted piano lessons. Then, one day, she saw a fortnightly series on learning keyboard—booklet and tape. She got a small keyboard for less than $100 and started collecting the series. She soon outgrew the keyboard, booklets, and tapes. But then she got a paid part-time job over one summer and earned enough to buy a beautiful piano. Her piano teacher friend gave her lessons in exchange for her having her ironing done.

Someone else wanted horse riding lessons and she used a gift of money to fulfil her childhood dream. She would go out each week for her lesson, her pockets bulging with carrots and apple to treat her 'friends'. Her lessons developed into short pony treks which filled her spirit and gave her so much pleasure.

So with this thought in mind, ask yourself:

4. *Do I have dreams to fulfil and how can I fulfil those dreams?*

Remember that it's *never* too late to do those things you always wanted to do. If you want it, you can work towards it.

The home education pioneer, John Holt, very much wanted

to learn how to play the cello. He started taking lessons when he was in his forties and he became a very good cellist. You can read his wonderfully inspirational story in his book, *Never Too Late*.

SUMMARY

This chapter has been devoted to considering how you take care of yourself. The answers to these questions are totally private to you and whoever you want to share them with. Their value lies in the thinking that you have done to get the answers and the changes you will make in response to the answers.

A lot of women find it hard to be kind to themselves or to spend money and time on themselves. It's false economy of course. And one of the things I hope to teach you is that it is prudent to take care of yourself.

This thinking and these answers set you up for being able to make quick and easy decisions about the type of homeschooling you want to have, and the curriculum you want to purchase.

ASSIGNMENT

1. Spend time answering the questions in this chapter. Consider how you can make sure you have a balanced life as you *take time to take care of your children's mother*.

2. Continue with reading any of the books I recommended to you in the last chapter.

3. Try to include art time with the children at some time this week. Painting, drawing, crafts, anything, as long as the children have a formal opportunity to be creative. If this is too much, then leave it for now.

CHAPTER 8
WHY CURRICULUM DOESN'T MATTER

For the past three chapters you have been encouraged to think and read around the idea of having a dream and a vision for your family homeschooling.

When you have a vision, you have the 'why' questions answered.

And when you have your vision, you can work out what your goal is.

Once you have your goal, you can *aim* for it.

The time you have spent on thinking deeply about the questions and writing down your answers means that your homeschool adventure is assured of success and happiness. And that's really where you want to be.

Taking care of yourself is fundamental on this journey, as homeschooling can be very intense, and you will be spending a large part of your waking life with your children.

Remember that when you are 'full' you can pour yourself out for your family, but if you are struggling or empty or have lost direction then you are like an empty jug trying to pour yourself out for your family. There's nothing there and the family then starts to suffer.

In this chapter we are going to look at the importance (or not) of curriculum.

YOUR TIMETABLE

Last chapter you added art to your timetable. In this chapter you just need to continue with your timetable, without anything extra being added. There will be more to come later.

If you want some fun classical music, what about some Gilbert and Sullivan? Try *The Mikado*—shortened version, or highlights. There are some very catchy songs to learn and join in with. And the story is entertaining, so the children are very likely to enjoy it.

AN IMPORTANT LITTLE HISTORY LESSON

Did you know that homeschooling isn't new?

A lot of people think that homeschooling is quite new and recent, but in actual fact, this is a fallacy. It's not *home* education which is new. It's *compulsory* education which is new.

What I am about to say next is very important. When you get a good understanding of this information, it will change how you decide what you want your child to learn and how you approach choosing curriculum for your child. It's fundamental to you

The first country in the world to introduce the modern model of universal compulsory education was Prussia (modern-day Germany) in 1763.

Massachusetts made education compulsory in 1852. And after that, many other countries followed suit. Education was made compulsory in Australia in 1873, in New Zealand in 1877.

Most other western countries followed suit between 1870 and 1890. This means that throughout the history of humankind, compulsory education has been around for only about 130—160 years.

Now the interesting thing to remember is that compulsory education doesn't have to mean school. And that's why home education is a legal, valid, and excellent educational choice in most free countries.

> 'Bless me what do they teach them at these schools?'
> C. S. Lewis, *The Lion, The Witch and The Wardrobe*

CURRICULUM

We don't know very much about home education prior to compulsory education. We don't know, for example, how many children were taught formally by tutors or by parents or were learning incidentally or were apprenticed or were working. But we do know that before school became compulsory, people had more flexible ideas of what was appropriate for children to learn and at what age and so on.

This is very important. So listen carefully, and I will say it again: before compulsory education, people were more relaxed about what they thought children should learn at what age.

The thing is, once we had compulsory education, we then had to have something to teach the children while they were at school. And that's when we got school curriculum.

Think about it; if you have children for five hours a day, over ten or eleven or twelve years, then you have to fill up the time with something; and putting that into some sort of order and quantifying the results is how we have a school curriculum.

So now, with the idea and knowledge that compulsory education for children is a modern social phenomenon, and with an awareness that different countries have different rules about compulsory education and compulsory subjects, it's easier to see that there really isn't any carved-in-stone-since-time-immemorial curriculum which all children should adhere to.

And with this thought, we can focus more comfortably on looking at the child, to see what the child needs, rather than creating a manufactured 'tick list' of 'compulsory subjects' that our children need to study.

KEEP FOCUSED ON THE RIGHT THINGS

Now that you know that curriculum is artificial and has little do to with real learning and more to do with ticking boxes of 'achievement', let me encourage you.

Be encouraged to keep working out what you want for yourself and your children. Keep working towards the freedom you want for your own family, and—this is important for your peace of mind—*keep your eyes off what others are doing, and what is happening in schools in your area.* That way, you are more likely to be successful and happy as a home educating family.

> 'Education... has produced a vast population able to read but unable to distinguish what is worth reading'
>
> G.M. TREVELYAN

WHAT ARE OTHER HOMESCHOOLERS DOING?

Over the past few years, certain styles and approaches to homeschooling have become popular for various reasons. Some methods are very formal and others very casual. Here's a quick summary on the more common styles, starting with formal and heading towards informal:

TEXTBOOKS this includes things like *School of Tomorrow*, Abeka, Bob Jones, etc. The advantage of this approach is that the parent knows exactly what to do next, when following the curriculum.

CLASSICAL EDUCATION as in The Bluedorn family's curriculum, or Dorothy Sayers' *Lost Tools of Learning*, or even *The Well-Trained Mind*.

It consists of the trivium, which covers
- Grammar stage (age approx 6—10) memorising and collecting information
- Dialectic stage (age approx 11—14) logic, discussion, drawing conclusions
- Rhetoric stage (age approx 15 or 16) eloquent and persuasive

UNIT STUDIES This covers programmes like *Five in a Row* for under-nines, also Weaver, Konos, Amanda Bennet's unit studies. The advantage to this approach is that it can be a lot of fun, children learn a lot of facts incidentally, and a few children of different ages can often work together. The disadvantage is that the parent/teacher often spends a long time in preparation, and it's probably she who learns most, rather than the children.

CHARLOTTE MASON This is based on the writings of an English teacher who lived from 1842 to 1923. Charlotte Mason put a lot of store by books and original sources in preference to textbooks. And because of this people may sometimes refer to 'living books' as a 'method of homeschooling'. The disadvantage to this approach is that Charlotte Mason's own work is not easy to read because of its antiquated style, so people rely on the filter of someone else who has read the work, and has worked out their own approach to using Miss Mason's work. This can be overcome by reading my book, *Charlotte Mason Made Easy*. In this book I write about an aspect of Charlotte Mason's philosophy, and then include some pages from Miss Mason's books, so that you have carefully curated, bite-sized pieces of Miss Mason's work. (www.CharlotteMasonMadeEasy.com)

DELAYED ACADEMICS (sometimes called the *Moores' Method*) This approach relies on the research and writings of Dr Raymond and Dorothy Moore; sometimes called the 'grandparents of homeschooling'. Their research indicates that waiting until a child is older before introducing formal academics is better for the child in many different ways. The Moores, also advocate a three-pronged approach of 'academics, service and work' in teaching.

UNSCHOOLING This is an unstructured approach, but it doesn't mean hands off, or uninvolved parents, or children not being taught anything at all. It demands quite a lot from the parent if it is being done well.

The interests of the child would guide and direct what is being taught, with the child being very involved in the voyage of discovery, and the parent acting as facilitator. The idea is that children learn best when they are happy and when they want to learn. Contrary to the idea that an unschooled child won't learn any academics, children who are unschooled well can be very capable, confident, and knowledgeable.

> *'Childhood is not a preparation for adulthood – it is a part of life.'*
>
> A.S. NEILL

WHERE DO YOU FIT IN?

A few people will know exactly where they fit in and what they want to do. Their children will co-operate and off they go.

A lot of others will try one style and when it doesn't seem to work, they will hop to another style, and so on, hoping to find the style that 'fits'.

Most people will feel panic-stricken because they don't know where they fit in.

WHAT DO I RECOMMEND?

I recommend that you think in terms of formal or informal. What style appeals to you? What happens in your family that you like?

Then read around the subject and style that appeals to you and see if anything 'calls' you. This will be your jumping off place so that you can find your own place on the continuum of formal to informal.

Be careful not to try and slot yourself into a particular type of education. And be extra careful that you don't accidentally slip into trying to incorporate all the best bits of various philosophies. You just won't be able to do it, and you will start heading towards confusion and burnout.

It's only by reading around the subject, and thinking, talking, and maybe praying, that you will eventually decide what sort of a homeschooling family you are and which way you want to go.

Then you will be ready to buy something. But before you pull out your credit card...

BEFORE YOU BUY CURRICULUM

First, I would recommend that before you spend any money on curriculum, equipment or books for children, you first of all acquire a few top-quality books *for your own bookshelf*.

Then I would recommend that you take the time to actually read the books. When you read them, have a pencil in your hand and a notebook nearby. Mark your books, make notes in them. Make notes about them.

Even if you have been home educating for a while, it is a good idea to reassess things in this way once in a while and regain your focus and passion if you are feeling a bit drained.

> *'I never teach my pupils; I only attempt to provide the conditions in which they can learn.'*
>
> ALBERT EINSTEIN

Refreshing yourself like this and having a clear overview of various methods and philosophies of home education can inspire you and remind you of what you want to do in educating your children.

SUMMARY

- In this chapter you have learnt something of the history of education as it relates to home education.
- You have an overview of homeschooling styles, with lots of guidance on how to work out what your own style is. And you have lots of tips about what to look for and how to make decisions on this subject.
- You also have another music recommendation that you might like to try and see if it suits you and yours.

ASSIGNMENT

1. Read widely on the subject of styles of homeschooling. Make notes for yourself to help you decide how you are going to be homeschooling in the long term.
2. Keep very focused on your timetable. By now it should be close to 'second nature'.
3. Try the music suggestion. If you don't like the music I suggested, just look for other music that you prefer. The important thing is that you are playing some good music in your home each day.

CHAPTER 9
WHY YOU MIGHT NEED TO LET GO
OF THE GOOD THINGS

What's the difference between a vision and a goal?

For the past three chapters you have been encouraged to think and read around the idea of having a vision for your family homeschooling.

And now that you have your vision, you can work out what your goals are.

This time that you are spending on your vision and now on your goals, is time well spent. It means that your homeschool adventure is *assured of success and happiness*.

We'll have a quick look at your timetable, then we'll consider the importance (or not) of curriculum.

YOUR TIMETABLE

With a chapter a week, you will now have completed six weeks of homeschooling. By now it should be feeling quite comfortable and your children will be in the swing of it.

Take some time to sit down with your children this week and look at how much work you have done. See how far you have come, encourage your children with their efforts and help them to see that you are all working well and producing good work. Then spend an afternoon or morning doing something refreshing and fun as a reward for keeping the timetable.

Even if you have failed several times along the way, you still need to reward yourselves for trying hard, and especially for starting again each time it went wrong.

WHAT CAN RAPIDLY DRAIN YOUR RESOURCES?

Believe it or not, the thing I am going to talk about now is something that looks really good, but which can be a huge drain on finances, time, and energy if it is allowed to get out of hand.

It's the number of activities that your child attends out of the home. I will call these activities 'out of home activities'. This includes all sorts of things like gym, team sports, dancing, language lessons, choir, homeschool co-op, writing classes, etc. Basically, it's anything at all that your child leaves the house for.

> *When you have a vision you have the 'why' questions answered.*
> *When you have a goal you have something to aim for.*

WHY HAVE OUT-OF-HOME ACTIVITIES?

If you are like most homeschooling mothers, you will be concerned to give your child all the opportunities that you possibly can. This is usual because we do want to give our children a rich and full education.

DOES SOCIALISATION MATTER?

Some people believe that if a child is not in school, he will not be able to relate well to his peers, or socialise with friends, or co-operate in a group.

Homeschoolers are often questioned about socialisation, and most homeschooling parents do consider this question carefully before embarking on homeschooling. What they find is that socialisation just not a problem for homeschoolers.

Of course, you only need to do a little bit of research to discover that homeschooled children have no problem socialising. In fact, we often see that homeschooled children are well-balanced, sociable young people. And to back them up there are literally dozens of surveys which all show that homeschooling is a good choice and socialisation is not a problem.

ARE ADULT HOMESCHOOLERS SOCIALISED?

I thought it would be encouraging to look at one study which was commissioned by the HSLDA (Home School Legal Defence Association in USA). This study is interesting because it looks at adults who were homeschooled. So it is looking a bigger picture, which I like, and I think is more relevant.

In 2003, Dr Brian Ray of the National Home Education Research Institute surveyed over 7,300 adults who were homeschooled. Over 5,000 of these had been home educated at least seven years.

His results were very interesting. They showed a group of people who were pretty settled, enjoyed life, enjoyed their work, participated in community service and were financially satisfied.

- Over 74% of home-educated adults aged 18–24 went on to take college-level courses, compared to 46% of the general United States population.
- 71% participated in an on-going community service activity (e.g., coaching a sports team, volunteering at a school, or working with a church or local association), compared to 37% of U.S. adults of similar ages.
- 87% were members of an organisation (e.g., such as a community group, church or synagogue, union, homeschool group, or professional organisation), compared to 50% of U.S. adults.
- Only 4.2% of the homeschool graduates surveyed consider politics and government too complicated to understand, compared to 35% of U.S. adults.
- 76% of homeschool graduates surveyed between the ages of 18–24 voted within the last five years, compared to only 29% of the relevant U.S. population.
- 59% of the subjects reported that they were 'very happy' with life, compared with 27 % of the general population.
- 73% said that life is exciting, compared to 47% of the general population.

The best statistic was that over 95% of these 7300 adults were glad they had been homeschooled.

THE BIG QUESTIONS

So if we are taking our children out to activities to broaden their education and to give them social opportunities, the big questions have to be:

1. *How do you decide what to take your child to?*
2. *How many activities a week are they allowed to go to?*

I have a friend who lives in the country. They are not wealthy, and for over a year, her children didn't go to any activities at all.

I have a friend whose children's activities mean that they go out in the car every single day. That's seven days a week.

Is there a middle path? What do you think? How do you get BALANCE in life so that you enjoy your homeschooling family?

Some people say one activity per child per week. I have done that in the past, when I had a baby and was homeschooling the four older children. And that worked very well. But as the older children grew up and finished homeschooling I was able to offer a couple of activities to each child. This was plenty. We still had time to do all the other nice things at home, and the children were able to enjoy the activities they did participate in.

One of the signs of an experienced and wise home-schooling mother is that she doesn't take her children out too often. They have time to 'be' at home. The children have time for PLAY, they have time to enjoy the home, to indulge in their interests, to relate to other family members, to grow in peace. So that home itself is a rich experience.

> *One of the signs of an experienced and wise homeschooling mother is that she doesn't take her children out too often.*

TAKE TIME TO ENJOY BEING AT HOME

This is so important. Often children are rushed from one activity to another, and they don't ever get time to just 'be'. It's hard for an interested parent to just to allow the children to be. To be at peace at home, getting to know who they are and try out their interests. It's hard because it can feel like you are letting things go, not doing your job right, or missing out on some wonderful opportunity.

But the children need it. They need time to process all the activities, they need time to think things through. They need time to play and assimilate all that they are learning.

They need time for imaginative play.

They really don't need time for computer games or DVDs or any screen time as relaxation. They may ask for it, and you may *allow* a small amount of it. But they *don't need* it. They do need freedom to play. Especially, to play out of doors.

> *Let home itself be a rich experience.*

MEETING WITH FRIENDS

When the children meet with friends, they need time to just 'be' with their friends; to work out how to get along together, without activities being organised for them, without games being planned, without interference from adults, or whatever.

Sometimes we have to let go of good and worthy things to

have the very best things in life. The best things can often be quiet time to reflect, enjoy life, enjoy each other and be at peace in yourself. And to remember, in these days of frantic activity, that it's good to sometimes just be 'human beings' and not always 'humans doing'.

CHECKLIST

Here's a checklist for you to work towards a balanced life of being at home and going out.

1. How many times a week do you go out?
2. How much does it cost you in fuel and class fees for your children's activities?
3. How many days a week do you stay at home all day?
4. How often do your children have time to just be at home without having an activity organised for them?
5. How much screen time do you allow your child to have?
6. How much outdoor play do you encourage?
7. How often do your children have time to play with friends without a formal reason for the get-together (like a class or a planned nature walk, etc.)?
8. How often do your children get to play with their friends in a safe, happy environment without an adult monitoring all conversation and play activity?
9. How often does your child tell you that he is tired?
10. How often do you tell your child to hurry up?

> *Sometimes we need to let go of good and worthy things to have time and space for the very best things in life.*

SUMMARY

In this chapter

- I've encouraged you to give yourself and your children a treat, as a celebration of the work you have done over the past few weeks.
- I've discussed socialization—its value in homeschooling, and the results of a homeschooling lifestyle.
- I have challenged you to think through why your take your child out to activities and how to consider the value of the activities.

ASSIGNMENT
1. Work through the questions I've given you in this chapter. Consider your answers carefully and discuss this with other adults close to you if it helps.
2. Make decisions about when, where, and why you are taking your children out.
3. Make sure you have some 'at home days' in your week.

CHAPTER 10
HOUSEWORK AND HOMESCHOOL

This is your last week of your Eight-week Timetable that helped you get started on homeschooling. And in the next chapter I will start guiding you through writing your new timetable. By now, you will be getting pretty well sorted in the direction you want to take with your homeschooling, your family and your life. And you are probably starting to feel ready to make that new timetable. We have just one more thing to get in place; I am going to help you get your housekeeping into some sort of order. I am going to help you see that housework isn't a necessary evil before getting on with the important task of learning; it's actually a part of learning life skills, and you and your children can enjoy doing the housework together.

YOUR TIMETABLE

During this week, notice what is working well and what isn't working so well. If you are a visual person, you can use felt pens or crayons to mark your timetable in colour with what is working and what isn't. Maybe use green for go to indicate that this is good, red for things you want to stop or change, and orange for things you're wondering about.

KEEP A CLEAN AND TIDY HOUSE

Life is so busy when you are homeschooling. And the house is always full of people, so anyone might wonder:
- How do you home educate and still keep house?
- How do you clean and tidy the house when it is always full of people?
- How do you stop your children from leaving their stuff all around the house?
- How do you get your children on board and agreeable about helping with the housework?

A concern that some people have about homeschooling is

the thought that they will have to live in squalor, surrounded by science experiments and 'works of art'. Nothing could be further from the truth.

If you are a clean and tidy person you can still keep your house clean and tidy. In fact, it's a good idea to aim for a clean and tidy house because it's certainly healthier to live in a clean house and it's time-saving to live in a tidy house where you can put your hand on things as you need them.

I like tidiness, and I have kept a tidy house with five homeschooled children and a husband working from a home office. Let me tell you some things I learned along the way, which helped to do this.

TEACH HOUSEWORK AS A LESSON

We once had a whole term of Wednesday afternoons at our house as housework lesson time. The children were learning how to clean the house. We asked questions like 'Is it better to dust or sweep first?', and 'Which cleaner for which job?'

Mr-Ten-Year-Old read the small instruction labels on the cleaning bottles, used the toilet brush with enthusiasm ('It's like cleaning teeth!' he said.). He enjoyed spraying his sister with the hose pipe while he washed the drive.

> *'The entire object of true education is to make people not merely to do the right things, but to enjoy them; not merely be industrious, but to love industry; not merely be learned, but to love knowledge; not merely be pure, but to love purity; not merely be just, but to hunger and thirst after justice.'*
>
> JOHN RUSKIN

Miss-Five-Year-Old had a lovely time dusting bookshelves with a feather duster, zapping the cobwebs with the vacuum cleaner and playing at 'librarian' as she replaced books on the shelves while tidying.

A young person who shall remain nameless tried to hide behind the rocking chair and dodge from room to room at cleaning time.

And another nameless one moved at snail pace, didn't do the dusting very well and unfortunately missed the M&Ms hidden in strategic places for him to find as he worked.

When we did the big weekly clean-up, it would take about a

couple of hours for us to do a good basic clean-up, by which time we were tired and ready for a yummy afternoon tea, and a rest. Then the children played. What we didn't do one week we would tackle the next week or I would do later, and I was surprised how much we achieved in our couple of hours, each week.

PRACTISE THE THREE STEP LESSON

A key to this learning time was the 'Three Step Lesson' plan when teaching the children to do housework:

1. I do and you watch.
2. You do and I watch.
3. You do.

So, for example, I clean the bathroom basin while my child watches, I talk about what I am doing and why. I explain in detail all the parts of the job.

The next time, my child cleans the basin while I watch, encourage and give tips.

The third time he can do the job alone.

> *'Habit is a cable; we spin a thread of it every day and at last we cannot break it.'*
>
> HORACE MANN

After that I need to *maintain* his work by checking periodically, encouraging him when he does a good job and gently reminding him of any things he might have forgotten.

HAVE GOOD WORK TOOLS

It's a good idea to have good work tools; it makes the job more appealing to start with and is a help in doing a good job in the long run—good dusters, rubber gloves, spray bottles, lots of mops and cloths. Even a tiny tot can join in with a mister or a spray bottle of water and a cloth, wiping down the kitchen cupboard doors.

HOUSEKEEPING CAN COUNT AS SCHOOL TIME

Here's a quotation from *Homeschooling on a Shoestring* by Melissa Morgan and Judith Allee. I absolutely love this message; there is so much truth here, and, as homeschooling mothers, worrying about academics and wanting so much to 'get it right', we often think we mustn't disturb a reading child and we must somehow get as much reading and writing into (or out of) a child as is humanly possible.

Just look at this:

> 'Don't feel guilty about focusing on chores. They are not separate from your homeschooling effort. They are an important part of it. If necessary, let academics slide for a while until you can get your home under control. You need to have a well-functioning household for your children to get the most benefit from homeschooling. Yes, it's okay to interrupt a child who has his nose buried in a good book if he hasn't finished his chores.'

Remember: it's okay to interrupt a reading child who hasn't finished his family jobs. This doesn't mean our children are unpaid slaves, but they are contributors to the smooth running of the home.

MATCH THE JOB TO THE PERSON

You can do this in a variety of ways. You can allocate jobs and times for doing it. For example, you could set aside Friday mornings or Wednesday afternoons for cleaning up. Or you could do half an hour a day before settling down to study.

Give little people little jobs. Show them how to do the job, let them do the job with you watching and encouraging. Then let them do the job themselves and make sure you go back and look at the work to encourage all the parts done well.

> *It's okay to interrupt a reading child who hasn't finished his family jobs.*

Don't expect the job to be done as well or as fast as you can do it but do expect the best that your child can do. Include them and praise them as they go. Give them tiny things to do and then check up on them. Give them lots of positive feedback for all their efforts.

Make it fun by having special morning tea or afternoon tea when things are done, or you can have a treasure hunt with MandMs at the end of cleaning time, and then you can give out weekly pocket money.

BENEFITS OF INCLUDING THE CHILDREN

Having the children help with housework has many benefits;
- They have a sense of belonging in the family, sharing the workload.

- They appreciate it when others clean and tidy for them.
- When they play, they play more carefully, tidying what they have finished with and using rubbish bins when necessary.
- We have a clean house at least once a week.
- Many hands make light work.
- The children will know how to keep house when they grow up and have their own house to clean.

Learning these skills, along with cooking and sewing, how to use an iron, use a hammer, wire a plug, is fun, easy and so important. When the children join in and help with the housekeeping you are including an important component of teaching your children that they do help with the running of the home.

One of the joys of home education is that the children see 'real life'. They don't go out in the morning, leaving a wreck in the kitchen, bathroom and bedroom and come home to a magically clean and tidy house. They participate in real daily life and in keeping the house clean, cooking, shopping etc.

> 'I am thankful for a lawn that needs mowing, windows that need cleaning and gutters that need fixing because it means I have a home... I am thankful for the piles of laundry and ironing because it means my loved ones are nearby.'
>
> NANCIE J. CARMODY

One of the harder parts of this approach is knowing what a child is capable of. The younger children often manage to wriggle out of jobs because they play 'helpless' and get 'rescued' by older siblings.

To help you, I've collected a list of jobs children of different ages can tackle.

HOUSEKEEPING TASKS THAT YOUR CHILDREN CAN DO

Adapted from: *The Superwoman Syndrome* by Marjorie Shaevitz, this is a 'minimum' list. Some children will be more capable and willing, but you can expect that your child should be able to handle these age-appropriate jobs.

3-4 YRS OLD (Children of this age need gentle teaching and firm follow-through.)

Dress self (put on trousers, socks, shoes, jersey, coat)

Pick up and put away toys
Empty wastebaskets
Help set table, clear dishes
Put dirty clothes in laundry basket
Close doors in room

5-6 YRS OLD (Continue to guide and remind)
Set and clear table
Feed pet
Help put away groceries
Dust
Put away games, toys, clothes
Take out the rubbish
Water plants
Assist in meal preparation
Make bed
Clean out pet cage, box

7-8 YRS OLD (Children of this age like to feel 'grown up.' Tasks should reflect this.)
Sweep floors, and outside paths
Help with food shopping
Walk dog
Vacuum
Wash, dry, and put away dishes or fill and empty dishwasher
Help with meals

9-11 YRS OLD (Children of this age are pretty capable and can be very helpful in showing young siblings how to do things.)
Wash car
Prepare simple meals
Use washer and dryer with directions
Fold and put away clean clothes
Tidy room
Clean up bathroom

12 YRS PLUS (Children over 12 need and want to feel independent. Whenever possible, encourage your children to select tasks and the time they will do them. Rotate unpleasant jobs among family members.)

Mow lawn

Iron

Do laundry, wash clothes by hand when necessary

Wash floors, windows

Buy own clothing (with a budget)

Run errands

Clean fridge

Clean own room thoroughly (dust, vacuum, tidy, change sheets, etc.)

Plan menus, prepare and serve meals

Babysit younger siblings

Clean cupboard or other storage areas

The younger your children are when you start giving them jobs to do, the more likely they will be able to do the jobs that are listed on this chart at the given ages.

BOOKS RELATED TO THIS TOPIC

Helpers by Shirley Hughes. A good book to read to little people to help them to see that keeping house is a family activity and not a mummy activity.

Clean in a Minute by Don Aslett. The best of Don's professional cleaning secrets boiled down to under a hundred pages. Great for those faced for the first time with cleaning or anybody who wants just the facts.

Chores without Wars: Turning Housework into Teamwork by Lynn Lott. Realistic and useful, tells what the family needs to turn housework into teamwork. Instead of family members falling into stereotypes, such as super-mother and spoiled child, a family built on the principles of reciprocity and teamwork can overcome the drudgeries of housework and lead children to value life skills necessary for their futures. Through chores, skills such as cooperation, planning ahead, managing money, and contribution are learned.

The Lazy Husband: How to Get Men to Do More Parenting and Housework (Paperback) By Joshua Coleman. A readable, practical, entertaining book written by a former lazy husband who is also a clinical psychologist. If you are having difficulty working out how to divvy up the jobs in housework and childcare in your house, then this book might help.

SUMMARY

1. You have five good tips on teaching your child how to keep house.

2. You know the benefits of teaching 'housework'.

3. You have a list of age-appropriate jobs for your children.

4. You have a list of useful books to help you plan and teach this subject.

ASSIGNMENT

Look through the lists and see what new thing you can teach your child.

Choose one of the books and read up a little bit on the subject.

CHAPTER 11
MAKE A FULL TIMETABLE

> *'The key is not to prioritise what's on your schedule, but to schedule your priorities.'*
>
> STEPHEN R. COVEY.

This chapter marks a turning point in the book. You have done the hard yards on working out your plan. Now I will show you how to put it into your timetable.

This chapter is quite big. There is a lot to read, and a lot to think about and plan. So you might need more time than usual for your weekly *Successful Homeschooling Made Easy* time. But it will be time well spent, and you will be glad when things are in place.

Your new timetable will be more complete and have a wider variety of subjects and topics than your original timetable. But first you need to decide what exactly you are going to include in your new timetable.

LITERACY

You will always have this on your timetable. This is a basic subject that will be there all the time. The thing about this that will change is the actual activity that your child is doing.

You may be doing alphabet books and drawing for the six-year-old, and Shakespeare and essays for the sixteen-year-old. With all variations in between. The work your child does in his Literacy Hour depends on his reading ability.

1. **PRE-READING**

    This is for a child who isn't yet reading, but who is very familiar with books, enjoys listening to stories being read, and looks through picture books alone. You will be allowing time for your child to do lots of physical activities. He will be doing puzzles, playing in the sand, painting, using play dough, peg boards, board games, picture books, ideally no computer games at all, and HEAPS of outdoor play.

2. **EMERGENT READING**

    You will be concentrating on teaching your child the alphabet, phonics, and letter formation. The child will be copying your very neat, large printing, or writing over the top of your letters or dotted letters. He will still be having lots of the physical activities mentioned in 'pre-reading'.

3. **ALMOST FLUENT READING**

    This child will be copying your very neat, large printing and spelling. You will also be making comments to him about spelling and how spelling works. Teach him any little tricks you know to help him spell tricky words. E.g. tap becomes tape, cap becomes cape—the letter A changes its sound when the E is there.

4. **FLUENT READER**

    This child is fine tuning his writing skills. He should have good handwriting now, but he will be working on grammar and starting to do his own writing. He will be introduced to Shakespeare and poetry in a happy, relaxed way. Take a month or two or poetry and then a month or two of Shakespeare. He should be able to write lists, keep a journal, write a short letter, with help.

5. **PRE-TEEN CHILD**

    This is a child who is a fluent reader and writer. This person will be writing book reviews, short stories, letters, journal entries, reports, compositions on things he has learned. He will also be studying literature, easy Shakespeare, and poetry too.

6. **TEEN HOMESCHOOLER**

    This child is working semi-independently, producing longer written pieces, writing essays, science experiments, reports as well as analysing work and reading classic literature.

If you are feeling overwhelmed after reading this list, don't worry. Take a second look, more closely. If you take one section and look at it carefully, you will see that I've summed up ten or twelve years of literacy in six points. So please don't worry; you have heaps of time for your child to learn these things.

> *'The workaholic maintains a frantic schedule. He is consistently preoccupied with performance. He finds it difficult to refuse additional responsibilities. He is unable to relax. If someone you know exhibits these characteristics, he or she is probably a workaholic.'*
>
> BILL HYBELS

Back to your timetable: in Literacy Hour, as well as writing and drawing in his journal, your child will be doing other literacy activities, according to his ability.

If your child is *just learning to write,* you may want to type his 'story' for him to copy. You can also look for a free handwriting font to match the style of handwriting you want to teach your child.

For grammar, I recommend *Grammar Lessons Made Easy.* This is a three-month, online course. It contains lesson plans and detailed instructions, as well as information on grammar, spelling, and punctuation. The course is suitable to teach to children who can read, right through to early teens. Find out more at: www.GrammarLessonsMadeEasy.co.nz

When you no longer need to teach your child to read you can spend time on poetry and literature, etc.

MATHS

This has been covered in Chapter Three. I hope you're feeling comfortable with what you are doing. If not, go back and read Chapter Two again. You are already more experienced now than you were when you first read the chapter. So you will likely see different things there and get fresh pointers for what you want to do in mathematics.

SCIENCE

Set aside at least one long session, or two shorter sessions a week.

I have a whole chapter full of ideas on teaching science later in the book.

HISTORY AND GEOGRAPHY (SOCIAL STUDIES)

Start by trying one session of an hour each per week. Add another session if that works for you.

Often these two subjects appear together under the heading of Social Studies. And in many ways, it makes much more sense. One of the problems you will face as a homeschooler, is how to categorise a learning experience under one heading. You will find that when your child is learning something, you can put it under a few different headings—if your child writes a brief biography of Mozart, is that history, music, or English?

With social studies, you can include a wide variety of experiences and learning moments that don't fit into other categories. For example, a visit to a local factory or recycling centre are counted as 'Social Studies'.

Stamp collecting is an old-fashioned hobby, but it might appeal to someone in your family as a good way to learn about different countries around the world.

ART

See how it works to have one session a week. An art session will last longer than other lessons because it does take time to set things out and clear up afterwards, and also, children often don't want to be rushed if they are creating something. Remember to leave plenty of time to prepare and to tidy up afterwards. And expect your children to be tired when they have finished their artwork.

To begin with, allow the children to spend time with the media you have chosen. Time spent exploring and enjoying a particular art medium is very educational. There are so many beautiful types of media and craft supplies to enjoy these days, but an experience of the basics will go a long way. Here's a short list to inspire you:

ACRYLIC PAINTS Choose two colours or three colours for a single session. Vary the colours each week. Try having just black and white paints. Try painting on coloured paper.

CHALK Try chalking on a blackboard, paper, the path, or driveway (at a very safe time of day and with suitable precautions to protect your child—e.g. a chair or other barrier at the entrance to your drive). Try chalking on a wooden fence. On any suitable, safe, and legal outdoor surface.

CRAYONS are clean and easy. They are quick to put out and easy to tidy up. Give your child good quality, generous-sized paper. If your child is stuck for ideas of what to draw, give ideas and themes. Choose something related to what has been happening at your house lately. Or ask for a picture to go with the latest story you have been reading to your child.

When the picture is finished, and when it's convenient, you can paint the whole paper with a coloured wash. The parts of the paper where the wax crayon has been applied will resist the water, and the rest of the paper will take the colour. This makes a very attractive picture and gives a 'finished' look to the piece. Use a wash from the art shop or just try food colouring in water. Don't get the paper too wet.

OIL PASTELS These are very satisfying because the colours are so rich. They are also very messy, and your child will need to wear an art overall and have a damp cloth nearby. Try different colours and textures of paper to work on.

SCISSORS AND GLUE Practice with these is very useful in improving hand-eye co-ordination as well as allowing an opportunity for your children to express creativity. Birthday cards are good to make.

If you allow time with each of these media at the rate of three or four weeks on each medium, you will soon have a wonderful collection of your children's artwork to put on display. Make sure you label every single creation with the name, date, and title (if it has a title).

Later on you can find or design specific lessons or a series of lessons to teach particular skills. You can also spend time making an art folder to store the artwork.

FOREIGN LANGUAGES

A foreign language is *always* a good idea. And *five minutes a day* is better than half an hour once a week.

Checklist for choosing a second or third language:
- Do you already know a second language yourself?
- Are you willing to learn it yourself?
- Have you got extended family speaking another language?
- Have you got access to a teacher or teaching materials?
- Are you coming across this language naturally in your daily life?

These things point to an obvious choice for second language. Also, consider teaching Latin. This is a good choice because it is the basis of so many romance languages and it helps such a lot in learning and understanding English. People often call Latin a dead language. But how can it be dead when it is still used as the basis for much of modern science nomenclature? It's very much alive, and it helps us to better understand our own native language, as well as encouraging us in history studies.

MUSIC AND MUSIC APPRECIATION

This can happen incidentally, but if it's not happening already, then schedule *half an hour a week* on your timetable. You might wish to encourage your child to play an instrument or even just to sing. Singing together is good for the brain, the lungs and togetherness. And apart from that, it just feels good. And even if you are not musical, you can get recorded music that you can sing along with.

Younger children will naturally sing higher than adults, so take time to encourage this in your child. And children learn to sing in tune. Again, this is something that you can teach, or that you can get help to teach. What a gift to give your child to be able to sing confidently.

OUTDOOR EDUCATION AND PHYSICAL EDUCATION

Put it on the timetable to happen for at least 30 minutes every day. Let your children spend as long as possible playing outside. Walks, trampolines, ball games in the yard, swings, climbing frames, skipping and all other informal forms of exercise are valid, useful, healthy and to be encouraged. You might also decide to enrol your child at a gym class, dancing class, or for a team sport.

TECHNOLOGY

Unfortunately, technology is very attractive, even when it's not the best thing for the job. Be aware that when children start using technology it will make a difference to how your daily life goes, especially as the children start to insist on more screen time and are reluctant to move away from the screen.

PRE-SCHOOLERS This is very **un**important for younger children. Pre-schoolers don't need to play games which teach them how to control a mouse. In fact there is much research showing that screen time will disadvantage a young child's development. Instead, allow them to experiment with more low-tech, mechanical equipment, such as wooden building blocks, wooden tool kits, helping to cook, bake, and chop in the kitchen.

OLDER CHILDREN who can read, you can include some teaching software in your timetable as it suits. Learning how to use Word, Excel, Outlook, etc., is very useful. Let them learn properly how to use all the features so that they these things become true tools in their hands. Again, computer games have extremely limited value—their main use is that they keep children quiet and occupied, but some consider that to be too high a price to pay for some peace and quiet.

TOUCH TYPING is probably still a must. People who learn to touch type can type much faster than they can write with a pen on paper. And this is a skill, like driving, that almost everybody uses regularly, all through their lives.

Some people never actually learn to touch type. They learn where the keys are, they get fast at typing with two or maybe three or four fingers,(or with thumbs on the phone) but they are handicapped by not being able to touch type. It's really worth spending the time to learn.

There are lots of touch-typing programmes around, both paid programmes and free ones. The latest versions change regularly, so do a search online to see what is current for 7—11-year olds.

When you are ready to teach touch-typing, put it on your timetable as a *daily activity of about 20—30 minutes* until your child is proficient. It should only take a few weeks—maybe a term.

HOUSEWORK

Remember this is a learning activity. Look again at Chapter 10. This is part of being in a family. *A couple of hours' concentrated activity* a week should make a good dent in the household cleaning. Also set aside *two daily tidy-up times of about 15 minutes each.* One in the morning *after breakfast* and a second one in the *late afternoon* before starting the evening meal preparations. These tidy-up times will be a sanity-saver, trust me!

PUT TOGETHER YOUR NEW TIMETABLE

Because of the work you have done over the past two months you will be confident in what you want to gain from homeschooling in your family. That knowledge helps you make decisions about 'subjects' and homeschooling styles.

The past few pages have taken you through the most common subjects that parents want to cover with their children. You may have some other specific subjects you want to cover. For example, faith-related subjects are close to the heart of many homeschoolers, and I would recommend that you carve out a 20-minute slot straight after breakfast for this. And there will be other things you want to teach that are not in the lists in this chapter.

Now, with your notes and knowledge, you are ready to write a new timetable. Be careful not to cram too much stuff into your days, give breathing space, allow for children working slower than an adult. Keeping it simple and uncluttered helps to keep it fun and workable too.

Let your new timetable last for a month. After that you will need to tweak and rewrite it. And each month you can make adjustments.

Each time you adjust things, put the new timetable on display and discuss with the children why you have made any changes.

Gradually, you will find that you are adjusting less and less. So that you will be making only two or three timetables a year.

SUMMARY

This chapter has helped you focus on all the subjects you want to cover with your children during a week. You are ready to write your new timetable. (Next page.)

ASSIGNMENT

1. Work through this chapter in an orderly way, making notes against each subject.
2. Then allocate the subjects in your weekly timetable.
3. Discuss the timetable with your children.
4. Display the timetable in the family area.

CHAPTER 12
RECORD KEEPING THE EASY WAY

I want to show you how to keep records for your homeschool. It's not hard, and it is effective.

WHY KEEP RECORDS OR PLAN WEEKLY?

Even if the law doesn't require any homeschool record-keeping, there is huge value in keeping your own personal, private records. Let me explain and show you a way of record-keeping that is universal, so that you will produce records in a style that suits your personality.

No matter what style of homeschooling you choose, or how old your children are, there are ways to keep a record of your homeschooling progress.

There are a dozen reasons why you should do this, but for now, I have just three important reasons why you should plan and record.

1. **Planning ahead links your goal to your actions.** By this, I mean that when you have a goal and a plan, you are more likely to achieve it and therefore more likely to make progress in home educating than if you don't have any goal or plan.

2. **It gives you a focus.** If you focus on your daily task list (this is the traditional way that a time-management plan works) then you may be easily distracted from the work itself, and you are more likely to be completely distracted from your vision and goals. You will be in a state of 'reaction', responding to whatever is happening in the moment, rather than having your longer-term focus in view, with your actions set towards those things.

3. **It gives you proof** that you have actually done something with the children. So often, we don't notice how far we have come until we stop and look back at the ground covered.

HOW TO MAKE A WEEKLY PLAN

To start with, you might write down what you hope to achieve during a week, and then, at the end of the week, you will write down what you did actually do.

Later, as you become more experienced, you will find that the lists of what you plan and what you actually achieved start to look more and more alike, as time goes on. This is because you are becoming more experienced in knowing what you and your children can get through in a week.

And as time passes, you will be regularly tweaking and readjusting things to fit your needs and your children's changing needs and abilities.

PREPARATION

- Set aside time each week to do your preparation. Some people like to do this at the end of the week. Others like to do it on a Sunday evening. So, find a time that suits you, to plan the week ahead.
- Be realistic in what you can expect from your children.
- As far as possible, stick to your simple and manageable timetable that we have worked so hard on making in the last few chapters. You will find that the children are more likely to work well for you if they know what is coming up and you are firm about the timetable.
- If you have left breathing space in your timetable for 'life' happening to you, then you are more likely to be able to keep to the timetable.
- Remember, it's better to have a realistic expectation and achieve your goal than to have a high expectation and miss the goal, ending up discouraged and feeling like a failure.

RECORDING

- Each day: assess what was done during the day. Compare what was done with what you thought you would achieve.
- Most people find that they set their sights a bit high to begin with, so don't be disappointed if you didn't achieve as much as you had hoped.
- Make your daily task list for tomorrow, adjusting it according to what was achieved today.

- At the end of the week, make a comment or note to yourself to say how you think things went. Then prepare for next week.

CHARTS AND CHECKLISTS

Over the next few pages, I have some charts for you. You won't want to use them all. But choose the ones that suit you and work with those. Print them, try them, personalise them just for your family. And then USE them.

I have included the pages here, with notes on them, and I have a link to pages for you to print and use yourself.

Look through the pages carefully.
- You will see that these are pages which you will fill in before the week starts, to show what you are planning to do with your child.
- But you can also complete the pages as the week goes on, recording what you have actually done, as you do it.
- You could even end the week by summarising your week's work with the children on these pages.

No matter how you decide to use these pages, it's a good idea to keep your printed pages neatly in order in your folder. This is your paper record of what you have done. And you will need the contents of your folder for what I am going to show you in a later chapter of this book.

BONUS ORGANISATION CHARTS

As a little bonus, I have a small collection of organisation charts for you as well as the planning charts. You can look through and print the ones that might suit you and your family.

www.successfulhomeschoolingmadeeasy.com/download/useful-charts/

www.successfulhomeschoolingmadeeasy.com/download/weekly-pps/

> 'The way to develop self-confidence is to do the thing you fear and get a record of successful experiences behind you.'
> WILLIAM JENNINGS BRYAN, American politician
> 1860- 1925

WEEKLY DIARY

WEEK BEGINNING: _____

FOCUS THIS WEEK: _____

Trips or visits:

Discussions:

Miscellaneous academia:

> *This weekly planning page is ideal for*
> - *Pre-schoolers*
> - *Younger children*
> - *New homeschoolers just finding their feet in the first few weeks*
> - *Unschoolers*
>
> *Write in any commitments or plans at the beginning of the week and then add to the page as the week goes on.*

Skills observed:

Physical activity:

Reading and Video:

Projects:

Other:

www.successfulhomeschoolingmadeeasy.com/download/weekly-pps/

Weekly Planner with Tick Boxes

Week Beginning: ___/___/___

Theme:_____

Subjects /Responsibilities	M	T	W	T	F
Morning jobs					
Bible					
Read Aloud					
Mathematics (30 mins)					
Typing (10 mins)					
Writing					
English Grammar (10 mins)					
Art					
Poetry Memorisation					
Science					
Social Studies					
Latin					
Shakespeare					
Literature					
Bible work					
Drama					
Singing					
Sport					
Music Practice					
Library					
Parent's List					

This planner is a good planner to try using if you want a formal style of homeschooling with the children ticking off the work that they have done as each piece is completed.

There is also space on this page for you to add a few of your own tasks.

www.successfulhomeschoolingmadeeasy.com/download/weekly-pps/

Weekly Planner with Subjects

Week Number: _____   Beginning: ___/___/___

Child One *Maths* *Written work*	Child Two *Maths* *Written work*
Child Three *Maths* *Written work*	Child Four *Maths* *Written work*

Spiritual / Values Teaching	**Language**
Social Studies	**Science**
Arts and Music	**Physical**
Reading	**Activities and Trips**

> *This planner works well if you want to keep a brief record of what your children are doing. You can see that there is space for recording for up to four children. It's great to have an overview page, and often, all you need to write in a planner is the pages or chapter numbers or the book titles.*

www.successfulhomeschoolingmadeeasy.com/download/weekly-pps/

Weekly Planner

Week Number:_____ Beginning_____

Child One	Child Two

Focus for the Week: _____

Shared Read Aloud: _____

Music/Artist/Poem: _____

Bible: _____

Social Studies: _____

Science: _____

Activities: _____

> *This is an ideal planner for teaching two children.*

www.successfulhomeschoolingmadeeasy.com/download/weekly-pps/

Daily Tasks

Today's Date:

Task	Completed	Time Spent

> *This planning page is ideal if you have an older child who is working semi-independently or heading towards independent learning. You can have a half hour meeting each morning and lay out the day's work and your child can have the pleasure and sense of achievement that comes from ticking off work completed.*

www.successfulhomeschoolingmadeeasy.com/download/weekly-pps/

SUMMARY

In this chapter I have explained the relevance and usefulness of record keeping and I have shown you some charts and checklists to help you work out a record keeping system for yourself. I've also given you some bonus organisation pages for you to check through and use as needed.

ASSIGNMENT

Spend some time trying out the different planning pages and see which one you think will work best for you today.

Make sure that you keep some records of what happens in your family this week.

CHAPTER 13
EBB AND FLOW

One of the things just about all homeschooling parents struggle with is getting the right balance between work and rest, work, and play.

Most parents tend to err on the side of too much work. They are usually diligent by nature, with a strong work ethic, and this can drive them to want to do too much work, not enough rest, and not enough play. So that eventually, they head into burn out. Either the child burns out, or the parent burns out. And sometimes both of them do. This chapter is aimed at giving you information and guidance to ensure that it doesn't happen to you.

Throughout life you will notice an ebb and flow. It happens in nature, for example in the tides, or seasonal cycles. Plants grow faster in spring and summer (think of the weeds in your garden), and 'sleep' or rest in winter. Some animals take the resting so seriously that they even hibernate for the entire winter.

Ebb and flow happen in relationships where we get on very well with someone then things ease back for a while before we come back together, better friends than before. It happens as children grow—we see them having growth spurts throughout childhood.

EBB AND FLOW OVER THE WEEKS AND MONTHS

It happens in homeschooling and learning too. Sometimes the children are very receptive to new ideas and learning, and at other times, things seem to take a long time to 'go in'. The children are slower to learn, and they seem more tired than usual. I see two common reasons for this.

1. It could be because they are having a growth spurt; I've found that when a child's energy is being absorbed in a growth spurt, they find it harder to settle and concentrate than usual.

2. The children get tired. After six to eight weeks of academic work, you will notice them start to slow down and tire.

When your child slows down like this, I recommend that you work with your child, go with the flow. Some ways to work with the situation would be to change direction, slow down a bit, or take a complete break.

GO WITH THE FLOW

If you follow school terms, you may find that your children are tired at different times to the school breaks. If that happens, you will need to decide what you are going to do about it.

If you are feeling confident in your homeschooling you may choose to take a break for your family, even though it's 'school time' for the rest of the world around you. Good for you. It's good to look at your child, rather than a calendar. It's good to see when he needs a rest. It's not an easy thing to do, but it's wise.

On the other hand, you may want to keep to local school times; maybe you have another child in school, or maybe your spouse is a schoolteacher and takes breaks at set times. In this case, it's helpful to shift gear without taking a full break. You can do this by:

- Choosing a slower pace of work.
- Increasing the reading time during Literacy Hour.
- Making Literacy Hour and Numeracy Hour much shorter and morning teatime much longer.
- Playing board games during Numeracy Hour.
- Making 'Play Time' last a little longer.
- Starting or finishing half an hour earlier.

Doing these things won't slow you down, because if the children are tired, they aren't going to perform at their best anyway, and things will only end in tears (yours probably) if you persist.

WHEN TO REST

If you and your children have been working steadily for several weeks, it's highly likely that you will need a rest. So now would be a good time to take a break for a week.

> *'Happiness is not a matter of intensity but of balance, order, rhythm and harmony.'*
> THOMAS MERTON

Some people don't take a break when it's needed because they don't want their children or relatives or someone else to know that they are resting in case it looks like they are slacking off.

In that case, tell the children or the other people that you are having a 'games week' or a 'history week' or an 'art week'. Then stop all other academic activities and just make sure you do some games or history or art each day. You might take the children out for walks or picnics and call it a 'nature week'.

Be creative but be realistic about everyone's abilities and be kind to yourself and the children. After all, they have done their best for six weeks straight. That's a lot of learning!

WHAT'S THE ALTERNATIVE?

The alternative to taking a break is to keep going, of course. You may choose to carry on, because everyone seems to be making good progress, you have a good rhythm in place and you don't want to break it.

If this is the case, and you have been working steadily like this for a couple of months, then you are in a strong position for taking a break. And you will be choosing to take the break before you are forced by some sort of melt-down to do so. When you've all been working hard you will all be running slower—a bit like a battery running down. Even if you don't see it, it is most likely happening. And it's better to stop while things are looking good and none of you is exhausted.

> *'For fast-acting relief, try slowing down.'*
>
> LILY TOMLIN

EBB AND FLOW THROUGHOUT THE DAY

Ebb and flow also happen throughout the day, and it helps if you can be aware of it, prepare for it, work with it and use it to your advantage.

When the day starts you will probably find that things start pretty slowly, and then the pace quickens throughout the morning, with a little lull, when you take a short break mid-morning. After lunch, a lot of families slow down for a short time. Younger children may have a sleep, older children may enjoy a quiet time of silent reading. And you need to make sure that you get some respite yourself at this time.

TAKING CARE OF THE CARE-TAKER

Every homeschooling parent feels overwhelmed by the noise and busyness of homeschooling at some time or other. The answer is not to send the children to school, but to have balance in your day.

It's not always easy to have the children around all the time, but if you set aside some moments throughout the day for a quiet, peaceful 'grownups only' space you will cope well with the demands of homeschooling and you will set an example to your children of taking care of yourself and respecting your own needs.

KEEPING SANE THROUGHOUT THE DAY

It's quite acceptable to send your children to their rooms for a quiet reading time, after lunch, for example. Or maybe you will send them all outside for a playtime while you have a quiet drink and read for ten minutes. These sorts of breaks are not only okay, they are desirable.

Of course, if your child is too small to be left unattended, you can get an older child to take care of the younger child, or you can use your young child's naptimes wisely.

DEALING WITH INTERRUPTIONS FROM THE CHILDREN

Now, what if it's your quiet time and your child is being beautifully co-operative about learning? Maybe he is asking you to read to him or to tell him how to spell a word or something equally 'positive' and 'studious' and 'profitable'. Should you interrupt your rest to teach your 'eager beaver'?

My advice would be 'No, don't interrupt your rest time.' You will be a better parent when you are faithfully taking care of yourself every day. Respecting the ebb and flow of the day, and of your physical and emotional needs. You are into homeschooling for the long haul and you can't afford to burn out.

There will be emergencies and rare occasions when you won't be

> 'Sometimes it's important to work for that pot of gold. But other times it's essential to take time off and to make sure that your most important decision in the day simply consists of choosing which colour to slide down on the rainbow.'
>
> DOUGLAS PAGELS, *These Are the Gifts I'd Like to Give to You*

able to nurture yourself in this way; and that's okay too. I used to say to my children that they could interrupt me if there was a fire or if there was enough blood that we would need to go to hospital. But each child asking me, one after the other, if they could have an apple to eat, or if I would settle a dispute, was not a good enough reason to interrupt me.

One final comment on this subject: homeschooling gets easier the longer you do it. And taking your rest gets easier too. Once you understand its value and take it seriously, it isn't hard to take the rest you know you need.

THE BEST HOMESCHOOL THING I EVER DID

I asked some friends this question and they answered like this:

- Take Mondays off. This helps me to regroup after the weekend (I don't do housework on Sundays and I don't plan the week on Sundays anymore either. That's what Mondays are for.)
- Ease up on lesson planning and RELAX. We all enjoy lessons a lot more this way.
- I give my children several alternatives for schoolwork and let them choose the ones they want to do. This has helped their motivation immensely.
- I close my ears to other homeschooling mothers saying how great their children are doing and how far along they are. That always left me feeling like I wasn't doing enough, and I'd come down on my children like a drill sergeant
- I put the children to bed by 8:00 every night and get me to bed by 10 p.m. That way I can implement the second-best thing... getting up by 7:00 every morning.

SUMMARY

In this chapter I have encouraged you to set realistic expectations of yourself and to look for and recognise when it's time to slow down and when it's time to move forward.

> *'There must be quite a few things that a hot bath won't cure, but I don't know many of them.'*
>
> SYLVIA PLATH, *The Bell Jar.*

ASSIGNMENT

Consider where you are in the cycle of ebb and flow today. Work on setting realistic expectations for your children and yourself today.

CHAPTER 14
MAKE YOUR LIBRARY VISIT COUNT

This chapter is a practical 'how-to' lesson, I will walk you through a family library visit. If you are wondering why you might need a lesson in visiting the library, just bear with me for a moment. Going to the library isn't just a matter of piling youngsters and books into the people mover and coming back an hour or two later with a hundred different books. It can be a fabulous teaching and learning opportunity for the whole family; a happily anticipated highlight on your homeschool schedule, an excellent use of time and energy.

Or it can be an afternoon wasted. I've seen and lived through both types of visit, and you probably have too.

A BAD LIBRARY VISIT

The bad visits may make you wonder if you really need a library visit for your children. After all, you could do all your research online and you have enough books lying around to satisfy the need for reading. And you would be saved the embarrassment of your children throwing the library teddies around, falling down the stairs, posting books in the wrong place, and needing the bathroom when you are at the farthest end of the building from the toilets, and are carrying everyone's books and possibly their abandoned jackets too.

And not only that—what about your children's choice of books? There they are, grabbing vampire books when you want to teach *Little House on the Prairie,* or flicking through books on teen angst on death, divorce, and drugs when you are hoping for uplifting, challenging classics to inspire them.

AVOIDING THE BAD LIBRARY VISIT

Bad visits like these have prompted some homeschooling parents to abandon library visits for children. They make a once-a-week trip in the evening, and they choose all the books for the children themselves. The children don't even actually go to the library.

Personally, I don't recommend this approach. I see the library as a wonderful homeschool resource to be used wisely; a must-have in any homeschooler's schedule.

A BETTER WAY

There is a way to avoid the embarrassing, exhausting visits, and the unsuitable-for-your-family books. I'll walk you through some steps to guarantee successful, productive visits every time.

We need two things for successful, productive library visits: planning and organisation. If you spend some time beforehand preparing for your trip, you'll find that all your visits are useful, fun, and happy.

> 'A library is not a luxury but one of the necessities of life.'
>
> HENRY WARD BEECHER

1. PLANNING

BEFORE YOUR VISIT

Plan your visit to the library in the same way that you would plan any formal teaching time that you spend with your children. In other words:

- **Think of what you want to achieve** (a happy, productive library visit, a stack of useful library books to bring home, relaxed children, reading children... add more things to the list). Write this list and you have your list of 'objectives'.
- **Make a list** throughout the week of books you want to look out for. You might like to print a list for each child that can read.
  - Your list will include particular books on a subject, maybe you have borrowed these books before or the books have been recommended to you.
  - Your list will also include any books in the library on a particular topic which is of interest to one of the children at the moment. For example, you might be

looking out for books about helicopters or snails or lighthouses.

> Look for the library list template at the end of this chapter. It has a download link.

- Here's a link to a library list template that you can print for yourself and for your children: www.successfulhomeschoolingmadeeasy.com/download/libraryhelper/
- **Check your library online.** You will want to see which books are due back this week, and you may like to order any special books.
- **You might also like to check the library catalogue reference number** (the 'call number') for books on a particular subject. This will save you a lot of time when you arrive at the library, as you will be able to go straight to the right section to find what you are looking for. Libraries use the *Dewey Decimal System* to catalogue their books and I have a *Dewey* list for you to print here: www.successfulhomeschoolingmadeeasy.com/download/dewey-nos/
- **Give your child a library checklist** to help her prepare for her visit.
  - She will need to take her list with her to the library, as she will have work to do when she gets there.
  - She will be looking for particular books and particular subjects.
- **Have special library bags.**
  - Each child needs her own library bag.
  - She needs to carry her own books to and from the library.
  - She needs to have her library list in her library book bag.
  - The library bag can be a great tool for teaching responsibility.
- **Discuss** with the children what will happen in the library.
  - Make it a gentle discussion, and show enthusiasm in your voice, so that the children pick it up and start to look forward to their library trip.
  - They will be responsible for returning their own books.

- They will work through their library list.
- They will have appropriate library behaviour.
- They won't run round the library or shout in the library, they will look after their own bag, books, and jacket.

2. ORGANISATION

ON LIBRARY DAY ITSELF

- **Collect all the library books** from all over the house, including bathroom, kitchen, car, bedrooms, and under beds.
  - Have each child leave his bag ready at the door or in the car
  - If your child has a water bottle, make sure he has his water bottle ready.

> *'And my father always took me to the library. We were both book addicts.'*
>
> CORNELIA FUNKE

- **Get all your other equipment ready.** Baby equipment bag, buggy, baby sling, pen, paper, cell phone, library card.
- **Give everyone a ten-minute warning.** This gives the children time to visit the bathroom, comb hair, find shoes, jackets, etc. and make sure their library bags are at the door or already in the car.
- **Make sure** that you give yourself the time you want and need to get ready, brush your teeth, apply some lip gloss, change your clothes, or whatever you want to do. Then it's everyone in the car...
- **AND...** we're off to the library!

DURING YOUR VISIT

- **Get all the children to carry their own** library bags and return their own books. Younger children will be guided by you, or even by an older sibling.
- Make sure that **you** assign caregivers to the younger child; this will help to reduce squabbles.
- **After the children have returned their books**, check with each one that she knows what part of the library she is going to and what she will be doing there.
- **Have the baby in a buggy or a baby carrier**, and then

take your youngest walking child, discuss how to choose books with him. Help him to know which books he is looking for, and which library toys he can play with.
- **When he is settled** for a few minutes, let him know you where you will be and visit each child, one by one, check that they are finding what they came for and give them any help they need.
- **Work through your own list**, collecting books, CDs, DVDs, etc.
- **When everyone has their books**, it's time for leisure browsing. Guide your children to the shelves you want them to look at. Take a few minutes to browse for yourself. Take your time and enjoy your browsing time.
- **About an hour after arriving**, it will be time to wind down the visit. Start rounding the children up. Take a quick look through their choices. If you have prepared and planned well, you will have few or no surprises here. If there are some surprises, you might choose to wait until you get home to discuss it with your child.
- **It's at this point** in the library visit that you can make this visit into a total treat. We have a tiny café attached to our library, so after checking out our books, I would head to the café for a drink and another hour of reading and browsing through our treasures. The younger children would get itchy about sitting still for so long, so they were allowed to play outside on the plaza where I could see them, and they were happy and safe. By the time we left the library everyone was feeling mellow, content and satisfied. It was a happy afternoon.
- **Consider what your treat might be.** It will probably be different from my family's treat, but it's going to be something nice that suits you and your children, according to their ages and stages. You might call into a playground, or get an ice-cream, or pop to see friends for a few minutes. Do what you all like doing.

AFTER YOUR VISIT
- **Once you are home,** the children are responsible for bringing in their own books, bags, jackets, water bottles, etc. and also, to help you if you need it.

- **It's a good idea** to have a special shelf or basket for library books, so that the books don't get lost in the house somewhere.
- **Enjoy** the books you have. Each one is there on its merit, and there will be few or no books that have got into your house by accident.
- **If** a child has chosen unsuitable books, look through the book, consider why it's unsuitable, and then have a chat with your child about it. Explain kindly why it's not suitable and put the book ready to be returned to the library next visit.

The time you spend preparing for your library visit takes longer to explain than to do—it won't take you long at all, but it will pay dividends in terms of educational value, time, pleasure, and satisfaction.

SUMMARY

In this chapter, I have given you some clear step-by-step instructions for your library visit so that it becomes a useful teaching tool as well as an event to look forward to and enjoy.

ASSIGNMENT

Prepare for a visit to the library and then make the trip. Try to implement any of the practices I have discussed in this chapter that will make your family visit more fun.

Look at the two printable resources listed in the 'Planning' section of this chapter.

> *'I was a great reader of fairy tales. I tried to read the entire fairy tale section of the library.'*
>
> BEVERLY CLEARY

LIBRARY LIST

NAME: DATE:

Book Title	Author	Subject or Call Number	Notes

www.successfulhomeschoolingmadeeasy.com/download/libraryhelper/

CHAPTER 15
HOW TO WRITE A LESSON PLAN

I am going to show you how to make a lesson plan and give you some tips so that you can start working on making a lesson plan today. Once you have mastered this skill you will be able to apply it to any subject or child whenever you need to.

WHAT IS A LESSON PLAN?

> '[S]he who every morning plans the transaction of the day and follows out that plan, carries a thread that will guide her through the maze of the most busy life. But where no plan is laid, where the disposal of time is surrendered merely to the chance of incidence, chaos will soon reign.'
>
> VICTOR HUGO

A lesson plan is a way of keeping detailed notes on what you want to teach in a format that is easy to read and refer to.

A lesson plan for homeschoolers is very different from a schoolteacher's lesson plan. This is because, as a homeschooler, you have more freedom in what you do and how you teach a subject. Also, you are gearing your lesson to a specific child or small group of children, so you can be more precise in your descriptions and in your plan, while being more flexible in your subject matter.

WHY HAVE A LESSON PLAN?

Writing a lesson plan is a good exercise for the simple and important reason that it helps you to think carefully about what you want to teach and how you want to teach it. Also:

- It will help you to prepare carefully for a special lesson, or for the first lesson in a series of lessons on a subject.
- You can use a lesson plan for a complicated subject, to give you confidence in your ability to teach the subject.

- You can have a lesson plan to go in a folder of examples to show the sort of work you do or did with your child.
- You might have a lesson plan to satisfy a legal requirement to homeschool, should that ever be a concern.

WHEN SHOULD I USE A LESSON PLAN?

You won't need to have lesson plans for all your lessons. In fact, if you tried to do this, you would find that you were spending longer preparing for homeschooling than any time you spent actually homeschooling. So when should you use a lesson plan?

USE A LESSON PLAN:
1. When you are introducing a new topic. For example, if you were to be spending a few weeks learning about electricity, you might write a lesson plan for the first lesson or possibly for the first two lessons.
2. If you are going to be teaching a subject that you don't know much about and you want to be well-prepared. For example, if you wanted to spend a term including poetry every week, you might need to do some research and prepare yourself and work out how you want the lessons to go and what you hope to be teaching in the lessons, you will want to have a lesson plan in place for the first week or two.

WHAT DOES A LESSON PLAN LOOK LIKE?

Usually, a lesson plan has a template, and I have made you a template for lesson plans particularly suited to homeschoolers.

I will talk you through the template and you will find a copy of it at the end of the lesson, for you to print and use as you need it.

> *'It's a bad plan that admits no modification.'*
> PUBLILIUS SYRUS (100BC)

LESSON PLAN TEMPLATE WITH NOTES

Subject	In this box you will write the general subject that you are teaching. Sometimes it's hard to be precise; for example, if you are teaching your child about Mozart is this 'music' or 'history'? If you are learning about how an organisation like 'Trade Aid' works is this geography, politics, or ethics? So feel free to choose your main subject or write in two or three subject areas that this lesson will cover.
Title	Write the title of your lesson here. So you might write something like 'Prince Henry the Navigator' or 'Tricks that Make Multiplying Fun'.
Age-range	You might write the age of your child if you are teaching one child, or you can put in the age-range, if you are teaching this lesson to some or all of your children.
Lesson Length	Write in here how long you think the lesson will last. You can write your estimate in this box, and then after the lesson you can write in your actual time. As you get more experienced, the two times should get closer to each other as you get more accurate in estimating the length of a lesson.
Objectives	Write here what you want to achieve with this lesson. For example, you might want to teach the square numbers. Just write that down.
Vocabulary	Write in here any new words that are relevant to your lesson. For example, if you are teaching a drawing lesson you might have a vocabulary list that will include 'perspective', 'cross hatching', '3B pencil', etc.
Materials	Do you need any special materials for this lesson? Maybe you need the book you are reading from, and your child needs his picture book and crayons. If you are teaching about a country, you might want to have your globe or atlas nearby. Whatever it is, get these ready before the lesson starts. Better yet, keep these sorts of items in a readily accessible place.
Method	This is the main part of your lesson plan. Write down all your ideas for teaching the lesson here. Include things like asking your child what he already knows on the subject—'What do you know about prime numbers?'. This isn't a trick question, or one designed to humiliate and show your child what he doesn't know. It's to help you be sure of where to start your lesson. You might already know the answer because of some work you did together last week. In fact, that could be why you are teaching this lesson, today. If this is the case then you won't need to ask, but you might just state the fact.

Evaluation	This will say how you will know what your child has learned. Well, you can see the value of this in a classroom situation, but at home, things are different. You can see how well your child has learned a subject by the questions he asks you. For example, if you teach him about the Periodic Table and he discusses with you the atomic number of gold, you know he has grasped the concept of atomic numbers and the Periodic Table. But if he were to ask you why there were spaces and gaps, and could he colour the table any colour he wanted; you would know that he needs more tutoring.
Supplementary Activities	You might use this space to record any activities that your child might do of his own volition or any activities that you think about to extend his knowledge and understanding of the lesson subject.

SUMMARY

In this chapter you have learnt:
- Why you might need a lesson plan.
- When to use a lesson plan.
- How to write a lesson plan.

And you have a template for a lesson plan

ASSIGNMENT

Write a lesson plan.
- Take any subject or topic you like, choose something that you have been a bit reluctant to teach because it is different, new, or hard in some way.
- Write your lesson plan for this topic.

Lesson Plan Template

Subject	
Title	
Age-range	
Lesson Length	
Objectives	
Vocabulary	
Materials	
Method	
Evaluation	
Supplementary Activities	

www.successfulhomeschoolingmadeeasy.com/download/hs-lesson-pln/

CHAPTER 16
TEACH SCIENCE

A lot of homeschooling parents say that they would not list science as one of their 'strong subjects' at high school, and the thought of actually teaching science is daunting for them. They think that high-school biology is a muddle of kingdoms and phylum, cells and tissues, consumers, producers, and omnivores; physics is more complicated than the dreaded mathematics; and chemistry is a confusion of chemical formulae and smelly test tubes.

Others think that they can't teach science because they don't have a science lab or access to laboratory equipment. And a lot of people think that science is hard. I want to tell you that it's not too hard and that you are probably already doing more than you think. In this chapter I have some pointers to get you going in teaching science. And at the same time, you can learn with your child so that everyone can enjoy learning science.

PRE-SCHOOL TO AGE 7

With children of this age you will probably find that you are already covering science very well. Here's a little list of things that you can do that count as 'science'. You might find that you are already doing many of these things:

- Give your children as much time as possible in the outdoors. Playing in the park, in the yard, at the beach, by the creek or lake are all opportunities for your child to discover the natural world and learn about God's wonderful creation. These opportunities are priceless in setting your child up for understanding scientific principles.
- Bake and cook. Anything and everything. Just include your little person and chat about what you are doing and why. It will pay dividends eventually when your growing youngster makes you tea and toast one day when you are feeling very tired.

- Watch a caterpillar eating. If you are able, observe it through its life cycle to becoming a butterfly.
- Use a magnifying glass to inspect anything and everything at close range.
- Use a magnifying glass in the sun to melt chocolate—this shows the power of the sun and how concentrating the heat of the sun on one spot can actually start a fire. You can discuss how fires can be accidentally started in a dry forest.
- Make a volcano with vinegar and baking soda.
- Play with magnets and magnet games.
- Encourage your child to grow something. If you have a garden, then quick growing vegetables like radishes are always a great success as children like to eat what they grow. If you don't have a garden then consider what you can put in a pot on the windowsill—herbs, a spring bulb, sprouted seeds, nasturtiums...
- Keep nature programmes as a very tiny part of your science work. The programmes offer little value to young children in terms of understanding science and nature, and they do take away the magic of discovery in real life, and I think they sometimes cheapen beauty.
- Choose library books for your child from the non-fiction sections; look for machinery, how things work, nature, science experiments, and more.
- Consider an annual pass to the local zoo or science museum and plan to go every two or three weeks, or even once a month. Write it into your timetable.
- Look for a good quality magnifying glass. A magnification of eight or more is great. A jeweller's magnifier is good.
- A pair of binoculars that you can bring out when needed can really help to increase the enjoyment of seeing birds and wildlife . Choose modern ones that you will use and can teach your child to use under supervision.
- Invest in good quality field guides of plants, birds, and animals in your area. Remember to use them.
- Start a nature table or a science table. You can use a low bookshelf top or a wide windowsill or a table. This is a display area and can include all sorts of scientific discoveries like birds' nests, leaves, seeds, seashells,

fossils, and bones. Change the display regularly to keep it fresh. Make labels for things on the table using brightly coloured card and a thick permanent marker pen.
- Have tadpoles in spring, caterpillars in summer, autumn leaves in autumn, bird feeders in winter.

CHILDREN AGED 6—12

Keep up all or most of the things in the list for younger children. Also –
- Include a weekly nature walk for your children. This is where you will take a short stroll, observing nature, taking time to really look, and possibly draw what you see in a little nature drawing book.
- Encourage your child to try to 'think like a scientist', asking 'why?' and 'what?' and 'what if?' questions.
- Look for an opportunity for your child to enter a 'Science Fair'. Allow your child to do as much as possible on his entry and RESIST the very strong temptation to do too much of the project or direct the project too much. The learning and mental growth that goes on in preparing an entry is immense. And the prospect of displaying some work publicly can be a great motivator.
- Try to include at least one opportunity a week for your child to spend time outdoors focusing on an aspect of nature.
- Look online for experiments; *The Happy Scientist*, has experiments that you can watch, read, and actually copy at home. The videos are each about three or four minutes long; they are really clear and easy to understand and follow. I also like the *Brainiac* experiments on YouTube. Just do a search for 'Brainiac YouTube' and choose any one of the videos that you like the sound of. I *much prefer* the older videos—cleverer and more interesting than the later ones. I think my favourite one is the *Brainiac Science Abuse Test—Pass the Lunch Box*. And I enjoyed watching Jon Tickle walk on custard
- Try some 'magic tricks' from the science books in the library.
- Try making some electrical circuit boards. Once your child has made a simple circuit you can help her work out some

more complicated projects—maybe a warning bell, an alarm clock, a two-way transmitter... you will find lots of project books around. The problem will be that you will find yourselves spoilt for choice. So be careful not to acquire too much at once as you know it can easily become clutter (more about clutter in a later chapter).
- Rather than watch nature programmes, use your annual pass to the zoo and visit the zoo every couple of weeks or so. On each visit, plan beforehand which animal you are going to look at in particular. Spend some time just standing and observing your animal. Take a drawing book and pencil with you and try to draw pictures of your 'animal of the week' or 'plant of the week'.
- Keep on building up your collection of good field guides and use the magnifying glass to examine plants and insects.
- If your child is showing an interest in science, consider getting a microscope or getting access to one in a local college.
- If you particularly want a formal science programme, I have used and enjoyed the Christian series by Apologia.
- Continue keeping your nature table or a science table. You can include all sorts of scientific discoveries from an Archimedes Screw to an electrical circuit to a Molymod molecule display. Don't forget to change the display regularly to keep it fresh, and ask the children to make some of the labels for things on the table using brightly coloured card and a thick permanent marker pen.

CHILDREN AGED 11 AND OVER
- Keep on doing what you have been doing when your child was younger. Gradually some of these activities will drop off but some (thinking like a scientist, using the magnifier, binoculars and field guides etc.) will apply as your child grows into young adulthood.
- Encourage your child to read biographies of famous scientists. Books which tell the story of a great scientist are important because they inspire the reader. Many a scientist chose his or her career after reading about another scientist who changed the world for the better.

- Take a look at the life of a famous botanist, Jean Henri Fabre. There is a Jean-Henri Fabre e-museum. http://www.e-fabre.com/en/index.htm
- You will want to teach your child about the Periodic Table and about taxonomy which is the scientific classification most people learn in high school.
- Consider if you want to add a formal science programme to your curriculum. If you are looking for a curriculum which gives a creationist point of view, consider the Apologia books. If you are looking for a curriculum which gives an evolutionist point of view, you will find that any programme written for schools is likely to fit the bill.

RECOMMENDED SCIENCE BOOKS

Books go in and out of print very quickly these days, so recommending books is a risky thing to do. But still, I will mention a few books that many people have found very useful in homeschooling.
- *Keeping a Nature Journal* by Clare Walker Leslie. If you get just one book, let it be this one. I believe strongly in the value of observation to develop a scientific mind and this book will inspire you to learn how to observe. It's not a homeschooling curriculum book and it's not a textbook. It's a book which has value because of its excellent content, beautiful presentation, and inspirational qualities. You can learn how to start and keep a nature journal with your children. You can start a nature journal yourself and introduce it to your children no matter how old or young they are. This book will encourage and show you how.
- *Archimedes and the Door to Science* by Jeanne Bendick. A great science history story book to inspire your primary-school-aged children and you.
- *The Librarian who Measured the Earth* by Kathryn Lasky. A lovely picture book telling the story of Erotosthenes who calculated the circumference of the earth in ancient Egypt. Suitable for children aged 5—11.
- *The Periodic Kingdom*: A Journey into the Land of the Chemical Elements By Peter W. Atkins. The periodic

table has been called the most important concept in chemistry. This book helps you to understand it, by taking you on an entertaining and fascinating voyage through the Periodic Kingdom; the world of the elements. This is an ideal book for the older homeschooler to read in the study of chemistry.

SUMMARY

In this lesson you have an overview of the sorts of things you can do with different age groups of children to help them with science. I have given you some recommendations for equipment and books that might help you.

My aim is to encourage you to continue doing science and to offer opportunities to your child for him to experience the world we live in and to see observation and to see experimentation as a natural part of learning.

ASSIGNMENT

Consider if there is anything you would like to start doing in your science time with your children. Maybe you want to buy a zoo pass or start a home library of field guides. Or maybe you are going to start gardening with your child. Whatever it is, just enjoy the activity with your child.

CHAPTER 17
AVOIDING STRESS AND BURNOUT

> **STRESS:** *hardship, pressure, a constraining influence.*
> **BURNOUT:** *to burn until the fire dies down from want of fuel.*

Stress and burnout are so common in modern-day life that the new traditional response to 'Hi, how are you?' is very often, 'Busy'. People used to say something like, 'I'm fine, thank you.' Or 'I'm good.' But now, it's often 'Busy'.

There's a hidden message here, isn't there? There's an implication that if you are not busy you are not important. And no-one wants to be unimportant, ergo, busy is good. And if you are busy, then you must also be stressed and heading towards burnout.

This isn't true and it isn't logical. You can be fine, thank you, and happily busy, without stress or burnout. Let me show you how in this chapter.

Just about all homeschoolers take some sort of holiday or break from homeschooling. How about you? What are your answers to these three questions?

1. What do you do during those break times?

Do you spend some time during the holidays making it a holiday for yourself, catching up with your own friends, catching up on your own pleasure reading, doing some sorting around the house, spending time relaxing, spending time on your hobby?

OR

Do you spend time during the holidays taking your children to catch up with their friends, allowing your children time to relax, taking your children to summer camps or programmes, events, and classes that they are interested in?

2. While your children are enjoying holiday social times and being refreshed what do you do?

Do you spend time on your non-homeschool-related hobby, being refreshed and encouraged as a person?

OR

Do you make a plan to spring clean the house while the children are out of the way, and then make a head start on your homeschool planning and lesson notes?

3. At the end of the holidays do you feel refreshed and raring to go, looking forward to Monday morning and the new term ahead?

If you can put your hand on your heart and say that you have treated yourself as well as you have treated your children, that you have enjoyed the holidays and you are looking forward to the new term ahead, I want to congratulate you. I want to tell you that I am proud of you for taking care of your children's parent.

If, like many people, you are starting to realise that you have been mean to yourself and that you need to make a few changes, then read on

WHAT CAUSES STRESS?

We all have stress. Some stress is good for us. But too much stress is dangerous. I've made a list of the types of things that cause stress. See which ones apply to you.

- Life events—birth, death, unemployment, sickness, money worries.
- Feeling like you have no control over your life.
- Lack of job description and boundaries.
- Inadequate time to complete the things you need to do.
- Lack of recognition for what you do.
- Suppressing angry feelings.
- Expressing anger inappropriately.
- Comparing ourselves to others.
- Competing with others.
- Doing things for the wrong reasons.

To take care of yourself is to take care of your family.

WHAT CAUSES BURNOUT?

Burnout isn't just 'too much stress'. Burnout is a reaction to stress. It's the way we deal with stress that leads to burnout. So how do you know if you are stressed or heading into burnout? Some of the symptoms of burnout might be:

- Things that used to be fun now feel like drudgery.
- You feel more cynical or bitter about homeschooling and what you are doing.
- You feel easily annoyed or irritated by your spouse or your children or your friends.
- You might feel angry about all sorts of little things
- You feel envious of individuals who are happy in their work.
- You care less now than you used to about doing a 'good job'.
- You regularly experience fatigue and low energy levels.
- You are depressed on Sunday afternoons thinking about Monday and the coming week.
- You have a feeling of helplessness.
- You get headaches or stomach aches.
- You start seriously considering putting your children into school.

One of the attributes of parenthood, motherhood and homeschooling is that the homeschooling adult has many different roles. And that one fact can contribute to burnout. As it is often the mother in the family who is homeschooling, I will speak now, to mothers, but these words apply to fathers, aunties, uncles, grandparents, friends and all the rest. It applies to the adult who is homeschooling a child or three.

Self-nurturing may be the hardest task you'll ever do.

YOU MIGHT BE A SPOUSE

And if you are burned out your spouse is the first to know—in detail. This means that you will both be suffering. The problem here is that people generally don't find it is easy to articulate their needs and to ask for help. It is seen somehow as weak or failing. In actual fact it is failing if you don't ask.

You might be a mother

The mother is 'the safe place', the rock, the comfort blanket in your child's life. You are the nurturer, the cuddly one. And yet how many times do we choose to be the controller, the policeman, making sure our children don't step out of line. So take it easy and ENJOY your children. I am definitely **not** saying that we should not discipline our children, and I am **not** suggesting that you should try and be a buddy to your child. But that please remember to ENJOY the time you spend with them.

> 'The problem is not how much we do, but in the goals, attitudes and resources with which we do it.'
>
> L.J. OGLIVIE

You are a teacher

I see this as secondary to your role as the child's nurturer and carer, and it's important that you never slip into the false thinking that you have a little school at home and that one of the adults in the home is the teacher and the other adult is the principal. You are a *family*, in a *family home* which is a safe place and a refuge. You are the parent in the family and your children are learning at home.

> 'There's a time for everything and a season for every activity under heaven'
>
> THE BIBLE

You are a homemaker

It's hard to remember this when we get very caught up in homeschooling, but what you do and the decisions you make set the atmosphere for the entire household. And homeschooling can be time-consuming and emotionally demanding. So, if you are not careful, it's easy to let home-making slip down the priority list. Here's some tips to help you keep balance:

- Try to include the whole family in housekeeping.
- Look for shortcuts and use them.
- Don't put too much pressure on your oldest child if he or she is a good helper (always ask the youngest who is capable of the job you want doing).
- Get help. There is no disgrace in having a cleaner to come and help you with housework. You are not paying for private school, so if you need help consider whether

> The most wasted day is one in which we have not laughed.

you can afford to pay for help. Even if it's just for a short time to help you through the hard time.

YOU ARE A ROLE MODEL

You are a role model to your children. So you need to teach your daughters how to look after themselves when they are mothers at home, and one way to demonstrate this is to rest when you are tired. You need to show your boys how to look after their wives and how to encourage their wives to look after themselves. They will also learn that they, too, must rest when they are tired.

YOU MIGHT BE A FRIEND/DAUGHTER/SISTER

Don't forget about the life you have apart from your home and children. As adults, we need our own friends and friendships. They are important for both men and for women. It's worth spending time nurturing your adult friendships, so don't feel guilty about enjoying time out with a friend. During times of hardship, these friends will be your best support persons, and you will be theirs. This will be the place where you get recognition, approval, affirmation, and encouragement,— these things that give a sense of belonging, and help to stave off burnout and keep stress under control.

IF YOU DO START TO BURNOUT...

False ideas and beliefs about your role will cause immense pain and stress for you and could cause burnout quite quickly if you allow it to.

Here's a handy list of dos and don'ts for you to put into practice:
- DON'T compare yourself to any other family
- DON'T compare yourself to school
- DON'T try to imitate school which is trying to imitate real life
- Do set aside time to think and plan and prepare your ideas
- DON'T over prepare because you will then find it hard to be flexible when needed
- DON'T spend too much money on resources because you will feel obliged to use them even if they are not suitable

- Do ask for help when you need it
- Do remember that when you take care of yourself you are taking care of your family
- Do try to eat healthily; this will make a difference to how you feel
- Do take time out to have fun with friends and spouse
- Do try to have a little nap in the afternoon, especially if you have a child under three or if you are pregnant

IF YOU ARE PUSHING YOURSELF TOO HARD

Ask yourself
- WHY am I taking care of my children better than myself?
- WHEN am I taking time to care for myself?
- WHO will take care of me if I don't take care of me?
- WHAT happens when I don't look after myself?
- WHAT example am I setting to my children of how a mother, a woman, should look after herself?

SUMMARY

This chapter has tools to help you avoid or move away from burnout. Take note of the advice and information in this chapter. You don't have to go down the road to burnout. And if you are already there, then do just one tiny thing to be heading in the right direction, away from and out of burnout. Back to full health, and restoration of balance.

ASSIGNMENT

Take care of yourself as well as you take care of your children.

Take care of yourself every single day.

Do it for the sake of your children if nothing else. They need a happy, healthy parent. And if you are not functioning well, then the family suffers.

> 'Things do not change; we do.'
> HENRY DAVID THOREAU

CHAPTER 18
WHAT WOULD YOU DO DIFFERENTLY?

I am going to share with you what some experienced homeschoolers have told me about homeschooling. I looked for those who have homeschooled successfully for several years and I asked them to tell me about three things:
1. What they wish they had done differently.
2. What they would do now if they were to start again.
3. What they know now that they wish they had known then.

I know you will benefit a lot from listening to these experienced and wise homeschoolers. They have some good info and the info is here for you to benefit from. (Names have been changed.)

REBECCA
Mother of four children aged fourteen down to eight months.

If you were just starting homeschooling, what would you do differently?

If I were just starting homeschooling, I would start out as I mean to continue and not dilly dally around trying lots of different things and philosophies but never quite making it work because we got bored and moved on to something that looked more interesting.

I wish I had been able to get less frustrated and so be gentler in my manner when dealing with difficult and challenging behaviours during the learning process. I wouldn't waste so much money buying curricular materials that I rarely ended up using.

What do you know now that you wish you had known then?

Not a lot actually as a lot of what I know now I am glad I didn't know then or it might have put me off and then I wouldn't have had all the wonderful experiences that we have had over the years. Although it would have helped, I think, to know that everyone has tough times and we are not alone when we struggle but that these times of struggle are just phases and eventually pass.

What would you tell a new homeschooler, just starting out in homeschooling?

Don't try to compete or compare your children's progress with others and don't start doing sit-down formal lessons too young or you will burn out before you are really even started. However when you do start, make sure you have a good routine in place from day one. Use your children's interests to guide your planning and to engage them in their learning but be the one who has the final say in what you do and why you do it. Be gentle in your directions and corrections but be consistent in your expectations and applications.

Susan

Mother of five children aged twelve down to four.

I know what I am doing differently with my youngest two children, (ages 4 and 6) compared to the older children (ages 12, 11 and 10) when they were the same age, but part of that is because I have older children to work around rather than only the young ones...

What I am doing differently second time around:

- I use a maths curriculum right from day one—I was stressed about how to do maths and just doing numeracy and games etc., caused me unnecessary worry.
- I get them to read to me a little bit every day—but I don't stress if we miss a day (or three). I have a more organised library of books that are easily accessible to the children and a greater variety of books available.
- I do more Five in a Row books and enjoy the books more because I know that after these little ones I don't have the excuse to read these lovely picture books anymore (well not till grandchildren and that might be a while yet.) But I don't do all the activities and I don't keep a record of them in a book for future reference—I don't have much time for filing and sorting.
- Then I let them do what they want because I am busy with the older children. If they want to draw, then they draw (I don't do paints and messy stuff because I don't

have the time to clean it up), if they want to play, then they play (until they start fighting with each other and then I have to send one in one direction and the other in another.)
- I do much less craft, less games with the children, less extension of the activity they are doing, less educational outings—these were all great with the first ones, but I don't have time for all that now and so they do more on their own, but also they do some of these things with the older children. They have much more exposure to things the older children are doing such as attending choirs, orchestras, Shakespeare plays and homeschool group activities.

I think it would be great to do more with the younger ones if I had more time, but I don't have the time and they benefit from other things that the older children didn't have the benefit of. You can't do everything the same for all your children and the experience of being a younger child is not the same as being an older child, even in the same family.

TRACY

Mother of four homeschooled children aged eleven down to four.
What would you do differently?
- I wouldn't add formal academic learning into our home and the life of our children just because they reached a 'magical' age when they would otherwise be starting school.
- I wouldn't worry so much, especially about what others think I should be doing or what other schooled and homeschooled children are doing.
- I wouldn't focus so much on my eldest children and have our lives so ruled by their 'formal' learning needs.
- I wouldn't buy any curriculum except for possibly a phonics and handwriting programme (if you felt the need) before my children were seven or eight or even ten or eleven.
- I wouldn't stop going for walks every day and enjoying lots of time outside with my children because they were now that 'magical age' where they needed to do book learning.
- I would relax more and enjoy the journey.

What would you definitely do again?
- Start my children's life off with a sleeping and eating routine and giving them set times to sleep and play on their own.
- Take the opportunity to homeschool (and the privilege of being with my children from birth) and not send my children into any other regular care.
- Cherish the journey of homeschooling and all it has taught me, and how it has changed me.
- Nature walks.
- Read 'living books' to my children.
- Memorisation and recitation.
- Every day, I would take the time to sit down together to meet regularly as a family and pray together and read the bible together.
- Inspire my husband to read to our children.
- Have my children learn a musical instrument and instil the daily habit of practice.
- Have my children do lots of physical activity and time outdoors.
- Read and instil many of the ideas of Charlotte Mason into our lives and learning.

In Hindsight :
- I wish I had begun learning about Charlotte Mason and her educational ideas before having children or when they were very young—particularly her ideas on habits.
- I would have spent more time organising cleaning, cooking and 'home life' timetables rather than on 'homeschooling timetables'. And I would have involved my children much more in cleaning and looking after our home in a day to day way from very young age.
- I would have taken more time to teach my youngest three children obedience and immediate consequences in their toddler years rather than being too busy 'homeschooling' to deal with the little things that at the time seemed to be of little consequence or an inconvenience for me to deal with because it would take me away from the tasks and jobs that I had to get through to keep me on schedule.
- I would spend less time taking my children to activities and homeschooling events and more time at home and in nature.

- I would spend more time enjoying my children rather than worrying about all the things that we weren't doing.
- I would pray about my worries and concerns and issues and perceived failures, rather than reading another book or blog on homeschooling.

VANESSA
Mother of two grown sons both were homeschooled.
- I wish I had known about Charlotte Mason, and I wish I had implemented her philosophy from the beginning.
- I wish I had not started with my oldest son when he was not developmentally ready.
- I wish I had known that it's okay to wait to start academics until the child is at least six and sometimes older.
- I wish we had spent more time outside.
- I wish I had spent more time having fun teaching my boys, and not worrying about it so much.

WENDY
Mother of six homeschooled children aged 19 down to 7.
I wish I'd known at the beginning:
- That relationship is more important than knowledge.
- To trust that all of life is education and to remember that when the trials of life make formal book work impossible at times.
- Children are wired to learn and if we set a rich feast before them and encourage them to pursue it, they will.

ZOE
Mother of six children aged 17 down to 9
What would you do differently?
I would:
- Write down what my ideal day or week would look like and remember that it is a goal and something to aim for.
- Write down why I want to homeschool—I would ask myself:
  - What are the most important reasons?
  - What things are non-negotiable about our home educating, so that when things get hard and I need to

pare things down, I know what my skeleton is and I know what must stay in each day (so important when sickness hits, or another baby, or exhaustion). Maybe create something like a mission statement.
    - What I like about CM philosophy—so that when things start coming undone I know what to hang on to and why, when the children dig their toes in and won't work I know why particular things are important, and when I hear about other lovely things to do I can decide whether I want to include them into OUR day.
- Guard my rest time each day like my life depends on it—we used to have 'quiet time' from 1pm—3pm each day when the children were little as there was always a baby in the house or one on the way. It was lovely. The children had to stay on their bed (when they were seven, they were allowed to stay in their room but had to be silent). I slept usually, but sometimes read. It gave us all a lovely rest from each other and our activity. Others were surprised at the length of time, but we all loved it. When the children were a little older, they would sometimes play VERY quietly (they all share rooms) but mostly they enjoyed the time on their own reading or listening to music or stories on CDs with headphones or colouring or playing.
- I would listen to others who have home educated their children successfully when they told me what they struggled with and how was it overcome. In this way I would learn some of the pitfalls could I avoid or look out for.
- I would look more carefully at what we are reading and learning and combine our time more. I enjoyed the time we used to spend doing the same history etc. It was easier for me to organise in some ways and we would have great talks about what we were reading.
- I would be intentional about taking time out—if we were getting tired I would plan for a week off. We did that this year and it was wonderful. I would plan some buffer time during the year, rather than planning everything tightly with no room to move.
- I would keep close contact with a small group of supportive women and families. This is hard to do as we

have moved very often, but it's essential for keeping on top of doubts and the words of nay-sayers.
- I would try to be braver in making decisions. I doubt everything I do which has really made our journey hard at times. Sometimes you just have to try something, and it's okay if it doesn't work out how you had hoped. Then you can just try it a different way.

Advice to new homeschoolers:
- Remember that a plan is not your master. A plan is to be changed when needed, as long as the changes are done with clear purpose after prayer and discussion with your spouse or a good friend, and after reading your original mission statement etc.
- Avoid changing a plan because you heard someone talking about a certain book or curriculum which sounded good and works well for her family—don't be tossed about on the ocean of home education. Have a map and a compass and a crew to work with. Changes need to be well thought through. It is okay to leave good things in order to do better ones—and these will look different for each family.
- Spend time educating yourself—set an example for your children and nurture your own mind. Have books about home educating and other areas of interest (mine are home education, parenting, marriage and then interests—mission, craft, biographies, self-sufficiency...). Have a balance—home education and parenting are your 'job' so be well informed, but don't spend ALL your mental time there.
- Have a clear idea about what outside courses you can do for your children. We have six children so I knew that whatever we did for one, we had to make available for all. I did not want to be running hither and thither all week (we have one vehicle to share) and we all have a limited income. We said the children could choose one club sport from age 10, music lessons from age 8 and one other activity. Some of our children have not chosen to do these, and some started but did not put in the effort for music practice, so we stopped. It is a privilege, not a right. If they don't want to have lessons, then they don't have to.

- I appreciated reading early on that you need to accept that you will buy some books thinking they are perfect and you might not ever use them. Some money will be spent on things you never use. That's okay. Thank goodness for second-hand curriculum stalls.
- Remember that some days go poorly just because that's how it is, not because you home educate. Parenting and home education are intertwined so don't think that if they were in school it would all be better. It wouldn't.
- I sometimes think I need to brainwash myself. Others spend plenty of time trying to do it, telling me what to do with my children and why. I think that if I spent more time telling myself what I believe (and writing it down), then I would doubt myself less, and know why I do what I do.

SUMMARY

These women are awesome! When I read through what they had sent me I was blown away by their wisdom, their generosity in sharing their deepest thoughts, their willingness to teach newer homeschoolers.

ASSIGNMENT

Take time to mull over what these experienced homeschoolers are saying to you. Take on board what will suit you.

CHAPTER 19
WIN THE CLUTTER WAR

One of the things homeschoolers often struggle with is having too much to do. Most homeschoolers have times when they feel like they have too much going on in their lives and they need to sort out what they really want to do.

At those moments, they decide to unload some stuff but they're not sure what to unload or how to do it. This chapter is going to help you sort, sift, identify, and unload stuff that is hindering you in your homeschooling efforts.

IDENTIFY AND UNLOAD

When you are able to identify what is important and useful and what is holding you up and distracting you then you are able to devise ways of unloading these things and that will lead to more efficiency in your daily life.

When you get rid of clutter you will be able to make more time for yourself and the things you want to do, you will reduce stress in your life, and you will increase your enjoyment of life.

Let's start by defining clutter.

WHAT IS CLUTTER?

Clutter is the stuff that stops you from doing the things you want to do.

It can be all sorts of stuff—possessions, thoughts, activities, clothes, books... What else? Make your own list of anything you have that stops you from doing the things you want to do.

WHAT DOES CLUTTER DO?

Clutter robs you of life in four ways: psychologically, spiritually, relationally, and socially.

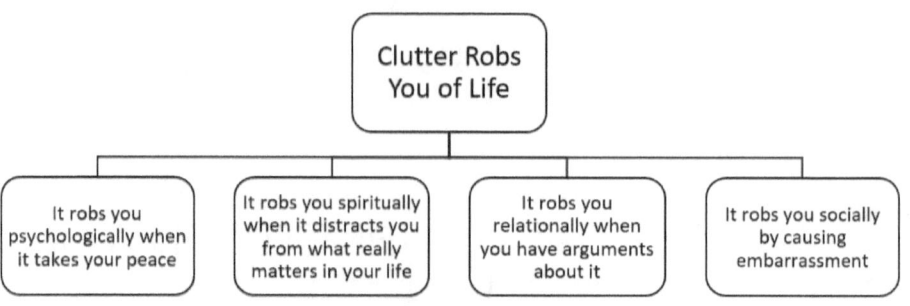

DEALING WITH CLUTTER

First of all, it helps to realise that the stuff that we own isn't the problem.

It's the way that we RELATE to the stuff that is the problem. So to deal with clutter we must first deal with the issues. And when the issues are dealt with, we can then deal with the stuff.

FOCUS ON THE ISSUES

According to Peter Walsh, author of *It's All Too Much*, most clutter can be categorised into two types of clutter.

- 'I might need that someday' clutter
- 'That reminds me of...' clutter.

Does this ring a bell with you? When you go to a cupboard or a drawer or a shelf to sort things out, you have good intentions about giving, throwing, and selling. But when you see the contents of the drawer, cupboard, or shelf, do you slip into saying either of these two things?

- 'I might need that someday'
- 'That reminds me of...'

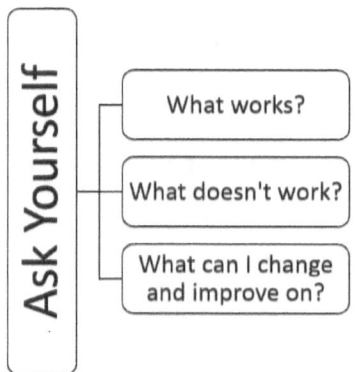

If you can work through this thought and decide on clear guidelines before you start tidying and sorting, you will find that your time is spent much more productively. So to start with, ask yourself what works for you? What doesn't work for you? What can you change and improve on? Then you can start clearing the clutter away, one piece at a time.

REMOVE THE CLUTTER – ONE BIT AT A TIME

EDUCATIONAL CLUTTER

This is any clutter at all that has to do with your home learning adventure. Three steps to being clutter-free in this area of your life:
1. Get rid of junk (what is junk? It's all the 'that reminds me of.' and 'I might need that someday…' stuff.)
2. Make sure that you don't allow stuff to overflow its designated area.
3. Equipment and books need to be accessible to be able to serve you.

CURRICULUM CLUTTER

Mary Pride is scathing about this and she says, 'Much of the stuff taught in school is not worth teaching; much of what remains misses the goal, and much of the rest takes far more time than it's worth.' Be very particular about what curriculum you choose to allow into your home for teaching your children. Choose carefully and take your time. If it turns out to be the wrong choice, then pass it on quickly.

> *'Your job is to pick the simplest way to present a given lesson and stick to it'*
>
> MARY PRIDE

LEISURE ACTIVITIES CLUTTER

Letting go of the reminders of leisure activities that you no longer make time for or continue to enjoy is a difficult task. Hobbies and leisure interests represent the person you want to be—more creative, more fit, more interesting. Old hobbies and leisure interests represent the person you used to be, and it can be sad and scary to let go of that person and those things.

When you confront the junk that has piled up because you no longer have the time or interest for the hobbies connected with it, you actually confront the changes in your life that brought about the situation. Understanding why you hold on to the junk can empower you to change your lifestyle and accommodate your interests or let them go.

NEWSPAPER AND MAGAZINE CLUTTER

Out-of-control piles of newspapers and magazines are among

the most common hotspots in the many homes. Remember that most of the content in newspapers and magazines is advertising material. You don't need to save old adverts. If you can't bear to throw out the magazines, then give them away. Alternatively, scan or cut out the articles you like, save those articles in a folder on your computer or in a scrapbook, and throw out the old magazine.

Paperwork clutter

Excess paperwork is the single biggest contributor to cluttered environments in homes and offices. Most of it doesn't need to be saved. Save only very important documents. If you think something isn't that important but it's hard to throw away, then consider scanning or photographing it, then throw it.

> *'If all of a given category of items are sorted in order of value, 80% of the value comes from 20% of items.'*
>
> Don Aslett

Sentimental clutter

What are some of your sentimental items?

How do these clutter up your lives?

Some of the most common sentimental items that we are most reluctant to give away are old photographs and personal letters and cards. By taking an objective view, you may find that some of the former emotional attachments that you held for these objects no longer exists, and you can easily let go of them.

Toys and children's clothing clutter

Holding on to toys and outgrown clothing can be a problem for many families as their children start to get older. There are several issues that must be dealt with.

- Why do you feel the need to keep these items?
- How well are your storage systems for these items working?

Teach your children how to sort. They need three boxes or bags to start with.

1. A box of things to sell
2. A box of things to give
3. A bag for rubbish

Wardrobe clutter

Most people do not use everything they own. Those who do use everything they own are usually men. Here's a question: why are you keeping clothes that don't fit, are old, or outmoded? You are not alone in this, but it's good to consider the question and your answer.

Wardrobe tidying tip:
- If it doesn't fit—throw it.
- If it is out of fashion—biff it.
- If you haven't worn it for a year—sling it.

> *Why are you keeping clothes that don't fit or are old or outmoded?*

Book clutter

Hear this from a book lover: Yes, it is okay to get rid of books. I have a set number of bookshelves in my house and when I run out of space I can't have another new book until I have made space by giving away or throwing a book. This makes me very particular about what I do buy, and what I allow to stay on my shelf.

Entertainment clutter

Are your music, movies, photos, games, etc. organised?

Anyone who has been collecting or inheriting music made in the last forty years could have vinyl records, cassette tapes, CDs, and MP3s in their collection. And as the record deck and tape player wore out and broke down, it's even possible that the person would have the same piece of music in different formats. How much of this is clutter?

Maybe it's time to rationalise your music, so that you just have one (possibly two) formats and junk the rest. Some people use only online music providers to listen online. That might suit you if you are very tight for space and have an excellent internet connection.

Linen cupboard clutter

Use your linen cupboard for linen and keep other junk out of there.

Bathroom clutter

Medicines and toiletries can soon clutter up the bathroom. Sort products according to their use.

Garage and shed clutter

Answer this question very briefly—what is a garage for? Hint, the answer is quite short.

What is in your garage?
- Unfinished projects?
- Tools?
- Paints and chemicals?
- Sports equipment?
- Exercise machines?
- Empty boxes from household items you bought a few years ago?
- Old or broken bikes, skateboards?
- Stuff you are going to sort out 'soon'?
- Stuff that doesn't have a home?
- Broken furniture, camping gear, etc.?

Tips for keeping your garage tidy:
1. Try to keep as much as possible off the floor,
2. Utilise wall space
3. Keep workspaces clear.
4. Have a place for everything.
5. Get rid of the stuff you know you don't need and won't use again.

Kitchen clutter

Keeping the benches free from clutter will motivate you to cook.

Make sure you have a good system for emptying the rubbish bins.

Have a simple cleaning routine—daily, weekly, and monthly.

Under stairs clutter

If you have an under stairs area, is it being used wisely or is it a great place to throw everything that you are not sure where to put? Get it cleared out. Decide what you will use it for. Don't let anything else go into the space.

Laundry clutter

Have shelves, hooks, hangers in here for all the various

pieces of laundry equipment that you use. Keep the floor clear and make sure the laundry is on your weekly cleaning schedule.

Computer and smart phone clutter

Do these electronics clutter up our life and take your time away from other things? I'm talking about the equipment we use daily. You might like to consider having a strict timetable for when you will use your devices and what you will use them for. Write it down and tell others. This helps to give you some accountability and support in your decision.

CLUTTER OUT!

Clutter is the stuff that stops you from doing the things you want to do.

It can be all sorts of stuff—possessions, thoughts, activities, clothes, books.

And because it stops you doing the things you want to do, it's worth spending the time ferreting it out and getting rid of it.

So identify what is important and useful and what is holding you up and distracting you. Create a vision of how you would like to live and how you would like your homes to be,

Then rid yourself of the clutter.

This will give you

- more time for yourself and the things you want to do
- less stress in your life
- increase of your enjoyment of life

And here is a rule for you as you work to clear your life of clutter.

The in-out rule

×	If you have to think about it, it can go.
×	If it doesn't fit in with your vision, it can go
×	If you haven't used it for 12 months, it can go.

SUMMARY

In this chapter you have been encouraged to unburden yourself and get rid of any clutter which is hindering you in your work as homeschooling family.

Spending time getting rid of clutter will be an investment

because you will be freeing up time and space for yourself and your family.

I found a lot of good ideas about clutter removal from: *How to De-Junk Your Life* by Dawna Walter and Mark Franks and *It's All Too Much* by Peter Walsh.

ASSIGNMENT

You know what you have to do, don't you?

But some good news—you don't have to do it all today, or even this week. Make this a long-term project so that you don't get overwhelmed and discouraged. Work on it one thing at a time and be patient with yourself. But do it!

CHAPTER 20
KEEP YOUR FAMILY SAFE ONLINE

One of the hurdles we face as parents is how to deal with things like internet, social media, and cell phones.

It is such a worry for that some parents might even be tempted to deal with things by keeping all social media and technology away from our children, but reality tells us that it's not a good solution. On the other hand, this doesn't mean that we should allow our children access to a computer and internet with only some occasional supervision. The best way is to be informed and wise and then teach our children how to deal with social technology wisely and safely.

This chapter is totally devoted to showing you how to teach your children internet safety. Your child is never too young and never too old for you to take an interest, inform yourself and apply appropriate safety measures.

> *We need to understand the basics of the internet, we need to be aware of what's available and what risks there are, and we need to be in authority, guiding our children from a position of knowledge and wisdom.*

LET'S START WITH A QUESTION...

How safe are you online? How safe is your family and your computer?

One of the problems of modern technology is the speed with which it changes.

For example, you probably know that YouTube was started as late as 2005. Mark Zuckerberg didn't even start writing Facebook until 2004. Google is really ancient—it was started way back in... 1995.

In 2020, Google, Facebook and YouTube are the most popular websites on the planet, but (apart from Google) it's unlikely you grew up with them.

So how do we guide our children when we have no model of how to parent children in this area?

The first thing we need to do is to be informed. We need to understand the basics of the internet, we need to be aware of what's available and what risks there are, and we need to be in authority, guiding our children from a position of knowledge and wisdom.

> *You must always monitor your child's internet time. No matter how safe you think they are, no matter how well you trust your child. It's not a matter of trust. It's a matter of protecting your family from unintentional objectionable material.*

Let's consider the risks for our families, and let's consider how we can go about protecting our families. And I'll also give you a sample cyber-contract that you can print and use with your child.

SOMETHING YOU MUST ALWAYS DO

Letting your children and teens use the internet can be a tricky thing. On the one hand, you want them to learn and be able to use internet resources. On the other hand, you may feel a bit uncomfortable about letting your children roam unchecked online.

While, I do believe that children need to be taught good computer and internet habits, there is one thing a parent must ALWAYS do. You must *always* monitor your child's *internet* time.

No matter how safe you think they are, no matter how well you trust your child. It's not a matter of trust. It's a matter of protecting your family from unintentional objectionable material. Once something has been seen, you can't erase that image. So the best thing is to protect against the image in the first place.

WAYS YOU CAN PROTECT YOUR CHILD

1. Educate yourself about the dangers so that you can take safety measures. I will talk about your options in depth, later in this book.
2. Have an honest conversation with your child about online safety. You don't have to explicitly talk about things like online predators. But make sure your child understands that not everyone online is who they say they are. Then you can come up with a set of agreements

about what your child will or won't do online. For example, they can browse informational websites like Wikipedia, but they agree to never talk about personal details with a stranger, online.
3. Have a contract between you and your child that you both sign. Having a contract is very effective and gives your child responsibility and ownership. I have made a contract that you can print and use with your child. You can see in on the last page of this chapter, and I have a copy online for you to print too.
4. Make sure that all computer internet access time takes place in the living area of the house and never in your child's bedroom.
5. If you have wireless internet in your house, you will need to ensure that the computer your child uses is not set up for wireless internet. A better way is to have a cable internet connection, with the connection available only in the living area.
6. Have a rule that your child doesn't go on the internet when you are not in the room.
7. Have set times for using the computer and limit the amount of time your child uses the internet.
8. Set a good example to your child by the way you use your computer, cell phone and the internet.
9. Discuss how to keep safe when your child visits his friends.
10. Talk about internet safety with the parents of your children's friends.
11. Keep communication open and chat about what is going on in his world.
12. Know what research he is doing online and be there with him when he is working online.

WHAT CAN GO WRONG?

By monitoring your child's access to the internet in the ways I am suggesting you will reduce the likelihood of your child stumbling into unsavoury sites or being lured by the wrong sort of people. I can think of lots of instances of the sort of thing that can go wrong.

For example:

- Some time ago a children's nursery rhyme page was hacked, and pornographic images were placed there.
- This took place a few years ago—some families trying to go to the website of the White House went to The White House 'dot com' instead of 'dot gov' and ended up on a pornographic site. In neither of these two cases were any children searching for bad stuff, but without protection, they were in danger.
- Something you need to be aware of is that there are online sexual predators who are out to woo children, groom them and lure them into danger.
- Children have also been known to accidentally give away a credit card number.
- Of course, your child could be exposed to crude language or sexual language.
- Your child could be bullied online or via text message, which can cause deep self-esteem issues if left unchecked.

But you can handle these dangers and prevent them before they even start.

MAKE SOCIAL NETWORKING SAFE AND FUN

I am writing this in 2020, and Facebook is currently the largest social network by far with over 2,500,000,000 monthly active users. The type of social media may change, but the message will be the same, so apply this idea to whatever the challenge is for you as you read this today. The danger of social networks comes primarily from how easy it is for people to get to know your child if they manage to make an initial connection. If someone gets in your child's 'friend' network, the social network makes it easy for them to come into contact again and again. Let me give you some tips for protecting your child.

SOCIAL NETWORK PROTECTION PLAN

1. Teach your child how to keep safe on social media.
2. Agree with your child about who to accept and who not to accept as a friend on social networks.
3. Agree that they must only ever accept friend relationships from *people they know in real life*, and never from strangers.

4. If your child is on a social network then you, too, need to be on. And you should be a 'friend' of your child on the network.
5. When you are on the social network you can check on exactly how your child is doing at any given time. Do this regularly; it can be a lifesaver.
6. Teach your child to always sign out of the social networks when they leave.
7. Photographs on Facebook belong to Facebook. Every time you put a photo on Facebook, you have given that photo away to Facebook.
8. Any comments your child makes on Facebook are there for the world to see, so be very circumspect in what you say and what you allow your child to say.
9. Help and encourage your children to make their Facebook profiles and information totally private, and I recommend you do the same.
10. Don't allow your child to delete his search history.

This is important for yourself as much as for your children. I once watched a chat going on between two women on Facebook. I was friends with them both in real life, but I wasn't 'friends' with them on Facebook. And yet, even though I wasn't 'friends' on Facebook, I could still read their conversation. Mrs A said hello to Mrs B, on Facebook. Mrs B asked how the children were doing and Mrs A told Mrs B how old the children were now and what social activities they went to. Mrs B invited Mrs A and family for Sunday lunch, and they agreed on a time to meet. Mrs A asked for Mrs B's address and she gave it online. She also said what time she would be home. Everyone watching could then see what time Mrs A and Mrs B would be out, and where they would be. We also knew the ages and names of the children and their social activities. That's too much information for a public place, in my opinion.

Another friend told the world that he was going to South America on holiday for three weeks on a particular date. It's not wise to give this information out so publicly, and stories like this, told to your children and then discussed, will help them to see why and how to keep safe.

HOW TO BLOG AND MESSAGE SAFELY

A lot of young people like to keep journals online. And some children might have their own blogs or YouTube channels. Others will post on message boards for things like games.

With all these things, it's important that they don't share personal details. They can refer to people by initials or by pseudonyms. And the most important thing as a parent is that you know where they are online, and what they are posting and receiving. If they have a blog, you can read it regularly to make sure nothing dangerous is being posted. If they're just posting about their new favourite music or their current opinions about a book or a course, they're probably fine. If they're posting personally identifying information or appear to be developing personal connections with people commenting on their blog who *aren't* their friends in person, then you might want to have a chat with your child.

One benefit of message boards is that they're usually open and easy to track. Just open the 'History' window in your web browser to see the message board posts that your child was viewing as long as your child isn't deleting their history. If they do that, then discuss why that mustn't happen unless you do the deleting.

If your child is being exposed to message board posts of a questionable nature, it's not difficult to find out. Once you do find out, then you should either have a conversation with your child about that message board or block the message board all together.

HOW CAN YOU DEAL WITH CYBER BULLIES?

Cyber bullies aren't out there to take advantage of your child in the way predators are– they're out there to hurt your child. Often cyber bullies are actually people your child knows in person. They could be children they know from various places who either have a grudge against your child, or just feel like they're an easy target.

Cyber bullying can sometimes be very difficult to stop from a technical perspective. They can range from people putting up websites voting about 'who's the fattest kid you know' to derogative emails and text messages.

The three helpful things you can do as a parent are:

1. Be attentive enough to know if your child is being cyberbullied. It's not always easy to see as children can be very good at covering up. A parent might notice signs like changes in behaviour, or eating and sleeping habits, appearing listless, withdrawn, or irritable or overeating. Watch for things like a change after being online or reading a text message.
2. If they are being bullied, to make sure they really, truly understand that the things being said about them *are not true*.
3. Try to find out who the bullies are. If you can find out who they are, take steps with the bully's parents to end the bullying.

TIPS FOR CELL PHONE OWNERSHIP

It's important to have some rules in place *before* your child gets a phone. If you try to institute a policy after they've had a phone for a while, your child will probably view it as a violation of privacy, and it will be much harder to get a policy in place. Some things you might want to consider when organising a phone for your child might be:

1. Always go for the simplest, cheapest phone for your child, and I recommend that you never give your child a Smart Phone or an iPhone. Giving them one of these is tantamount to giving them unfettered, unprotected, 24-hour access to the internet.
2. Decide together who will pay for the phone calls and texts, have a budget that will help to keep the number of texts and calls in check.
3. Ensure that your child isn't using the internet at a friend's house or sharing data from a friend's phone.
4. Have a policy of no secret messages. This will help to protect your child from bullying and inappropriate texts.
5. Have no secret passwords from Mum and Dad.
6. Have a policy of no cell phones in the bedroom at night. When your child goes to bed, your child will turn off his phone and leave it in the family area of the house.

Things that might ring warning bells for you and things you need to look out for are:

1. Your child spending too long or too much money texting friends.
2. Others sending sexually explicit text messages or images to your child's phone.
3. Others using anonymous text messages to send bullying and derogatory messages to your child's phone.

Have an agreement with your child that if they ever receive derogatory, insulting, hurtful or sexual text messages from anyone at all, whether they know the sender or not, that they tell you straight away

And then be prepared. If your child does come to you with this sort of problem, remember to KEEP YOUR COOL. Often, children will avoid revealing something like this because of the strong reactions they get from their parents.

Have a game plan ready ahead of time. Pull it out and show your child or teen that you are not thrown by this, you are not angry, but you are in control and can deal calmly and discreetly with the situation.

If you know your child is getting unwanted text messages, you can either try blocking the phone numbers the messages are coming from, (the phone companies will usually help with this) or change the phone number if you really need to.

SUMMARY

In this chapter you have been equipped to deal with some of the more common problems of modern technology for parents. However, this information could go out of date really quickly, so whatever else you do, please try to stay ahead of the game with technology. Our children learn fast, and they need our wisdom, maturity, and guidance as they grow.

ASSIGNMENT

Keep up to date on internet and cell phone safety, so that you are well prepared to guide your children.

CYBER CONTRACT
I Promise to Keep Myself Safe Online

I, _____, promise to keep myself safe when using the internet. I'll do this by following these safety guidelines:

▷ I'll never give out my phone number, my address, or any other information that someone could use to find me in person.

▷ I won't visit links to websites that I don't recognize.

▷ If I see anything online that I don't feel comfortable with, I'll tell my parents right away.

▷ If I get an anonymous email, text message or instant message, I'll tell my parents right away.

▷ If I receive a mean, insulting or hurtful message, I'll tell my parents right away.

▷ I understand that other people say mean things and that what they say about me is probably not true.

▷ I'll never give out my parents' credit card number online.

▷ I agree to never meet someone in person I met online.

▷ I won't download any software or .exe files that I don't recognize. I understand that doing so could result in getting viruses on our computer and put our family at risk.

Signature of Child   _____

Signature of Parent   _____

www.successfulhomeschoolingmadeeasy.com/download/c-cntrt/

CHAPTER 21
ARE YOU ON THE ROAD TO SUCCESS?

OR ARE YOU HEADED FOR HOMESCHOOL BURNOUT?

I've got a quiz for you. Quizzes are always fun, and I think you'll enjoy this one. I know you'll appreciate something lighthearted...

Choose the statements that best describe you, then tot up your scores at the end.

1. *Do you stop your homeschool thinking and planning at the end of the day?*
    A. Yes, always. I like the change of pace and I enjoy relaxing at the end of the day.
    B. Most of the time I do. Sometimes I get a bit enthusiastic and find it hard to 'switch off'.
    C. Occasionally I do. But I like to make sure that I am prepared for the next day, so I often work in the evenings after the children have gone to bed.
    D. No, not really. I have too much to do, and I spend the evenings getting sorted out for the next day.

2. *Do you start your day on time, according to your own timetable?*
    A. Yes. I have set our time for starting realistically and so we are always ready and able to start on time.
    B. I usually do. I have a realistic start time, and we manage it at least four days out of five.
    C. I try hard to start on time and usually end up shouting at the children because it's a very tight schedule.
    D. Hardly ever. I don't know what happens in the morning; time just seems to run away with me, and I find it hard to even get out of bed on time.

3. *Do you spend time looking at what other homeschoolers are doing and think that you should be doing the same thing because it looks better than what happens at your house?*
    A. I try hard not to look because I'm happy with what we do. I find that watching others or looking at what others are doing distracts and discourages me.
    B. Not usually. I sometimes look and I am tempted to copy others, but then I remember my own vision and I keep to my own goals. I do write down any good ideas that I hear about.
    C. I do sometimes look at what others are doing, especially if they seem very happy or successful. After all, I might find something better than what I have already got, and I want to give my children the best I can.
    D. I do notice that other homeschoolers seem to be doing exciting and interesting things and I collect information in case I might need it. In fact, I like to think that I am flexible and ready to try new things all the time.

4. *Do you ever buy books and curriculum that you like the look of on impulse?*
    A. Rarely, I try to only buy books and curriculum that I have thought about and planned to buy.
    B. Occasionally. I sometimes see something that I think it might come in useful when the children are a bit older, so I get it while I can.
    C. Yes. I like bargains, and I don't want to miss out on a good deal.
    D. Yes. I don't know when I might see this particular thing again and it might come in handy. I like to have a wide range of products and materials available that I can put my hand on if I need to.

5. *How often do you check your emails?*
    A. Not too often during the day; I keep away from my devices when I am working with the children.
    B. A few times a day. I check them at quiet times of the day but never when I am working with the children.
    C. Once a day; I try to avoid being on the computer and phone when I am working with the children.
    D. I don't know how often; I check regularly throughout the day because I like to keep in touch.

6. *Do you hop onto your Social Media pages more than once a day?*
   A. No, I check once a day, mainly to be in contact and to touch base, rather than to socialise in a big way.
   B. I check a couple of times a day; I like to see if others are replying to my posts and comments.
   C. I don't have time for any social time during the day.
   D. I check things out several times a day and I post often too. It's my social time.
7. *Do you set aside quality time, each week to spend with your Significant Other, where you enjoy being a couple?*
   A. Yes. We are firm about our date night and the children know what to expect.
   B. We try to have time together every week and are still training our children and working out the fine details of making this work, but it's worth the effort.
   C. We try to organise stuff, but it's quite a bit of trouble, and I don't like to deny the children, so if the children want us to spend time with them we give up the date night and have a family evening instead.
   D. What's a date night?
8. *Do you get to bed on time?*
   A. I'm pretty good at getting to bed on time because I know the value of a good night's sleep.
   B. Having a regular bedtime for myself helps me to function well during the day, but I don't always manage it.
   C. I aim to get to bed on time, but I like to finish things off and be well prepared for the following day, so sometimes I don't get to bed until late.
   D. I get so tired in the evenings I collapse on the sofa after dinner, and end up getting to bed too late, but I do intend to start getting to bed early soon.
9. *Do you ever read a book which is just for pleasure and not for any sort of self-improvement?*
   A. Yes, I do. I try to always have a just-for-pleasure book on the go.
   B. I save relaxing pleasure books for my holiday reading.
   C. No. I don't want to waste time; I only ever read homeschooling and parenting books these days.
   D. I don't have time for too much reading. I find I start books but don't manage to finish them.

10. *How often do you do something for your own pleasure and fun?*
    A. I try to have some space in my day every day when I can take a breather and relax, I also try to spend a couple of hours a week on my own hobby and interest.
    B. I am pretty good at taking a bit of time to myself regularly, although I still don't have it as a regular, scheduled event.
    C. I don't have time; I find that homeschooling, housekeeping, family duties all keep me very busy.
    D. Not often. We don't have the time or the money.

11. *Do you ever feel overwhelmed?*
    A. Yes, occasionally I do. Then I take a breath, change the pace, and start afresh the next day.
    B. Yes, but not very often. Although I take it as a warning sign, and I slow down and do what I need to do to get myself refreshed and refuelled.
    C. Sometimes I do. Homeschooling is a big responsibility. But I push on and draw on all my resources to get myself through.
    D. Yes, I often feel overwhelmed.

12. *Do you have 'home days' when you don't go out on any errands or to take the children to any courses?*
    A. Yes. I need days at home where we can just get on with all the lovely things I have planned, and I see us making happy progress.
    B. Yes. It helps to give good balance to life.
    C. Yes. On those days I have someone come to the house to tutor the children for me. I don't want them to get behind.
    D. No. I go out most days. The children like to see their friends and I want them to have a wide experience of different activities.

13. *Who does the housework at your house?*
    A. I allocate jobs for the daily chores and for the weekly house clean. I try to make it fun and give a nice treat afterwards.
    B. I am working on this. I am spending time teaching the children how to do various jobs and trying out different ways of allocating the jobs to find what works.

C. I don't involve the children in housework. I don't want to distract them from studying. I do the housework myself in the evenings when the children are in bed, or when the children are playing.
D. Housework is a problem. It's one more thing in my long list of 'I must do'.

14. *Are you enjoying homeschooling?*
    A. I love it. I am so glad to be homeschooling, it's a gift.
    B. Yes, I am, on the whole.
    C. I didn't really think about actually enjoying it. I am committed and working to do the best I can. I have a big responsibility here and I take it very seriously.
    D. I would like to be enjoying it, and I think I will start enjoying it once I have sorted out the problems I am dealing with this week.

15. *Do your children enjoy being homeschooled?*
    A. Yes, they love it. We all really enjoy our lifestyle.
    B. Yes, they love it. I like seeing the children thrive.
    C. They like getting the work out of the way so that they can do their own thing.
    D. I don't know

16. *Do you ever think about sending your children to school?*
    A. No.
    B. Not anymore.
    C. Occasionally.
    D. Sometimes I think they would be better off at school.

How many of each did you get?

DID YOU ANSWER MOSTLY A?

YOU ARE A SUCCESSFUL HOMESCHOOLER

You are doing an outstanding job. You have a good attitude to homeschooling, you are doing marvellously in enjoying homeschooling while still keeping a good relationship with other important people in your life and taking care of your own needs too. Congratulations and keep it up and remember to take breaks when you need them and don't push everyone too hard.

DID YOU ANSWER MOSTLY B?

You are a well-balanced homeschooler
You are thriving as a homeschooler. You know what you need to do, and you are working to achieve it. Keep on focusing on a healthy balance and enjoying homeschooling.

DID YOU ANSWER MOSTLY C?

You are a perfectionist homeschooler
You are trying to be all things to all people. No-one is Supermum. To avoid burnout make sure you give yourself and your children time to relax and just *be*. Remember, we are humans beings, not human doings. You might find it helpful to re-read chapters 7 and 10.

DID YOU ANSWER MOSTLY D?

You are a burnout candidate
You are on the right track, but you need to have more confidence in your own ability to succeed in homeschooling. You know what is right for your family, and if you focus on what you know is right and what you are learning in this book, you WILL succeed. I recommend that you re- read chapters 3, 5,6 and 10 to help you regain your vision. A good idea would be to focus on creating realistic expectations for you and your family.

SUMMARY
This is a fun quiz. Don't take it too seriously but use it to check that you are going in the right direction. And be encouraged to make any changes to your lifestyle to improve homeschooling and to enjoy your daily life more.

ASSIGNMENT
Find something that you would like to do just for fun. Something that's relaxing and not connected with homeschooling. Enjoy!

CHAPTER 22
TWEAK AND IMPROVE

When you are planning your homeschooling and using your timetable, you will find that having something written down does work. It helps you to focus. And if you have been doing the assignments in each chapter you will be well along in the habit of making and using a timetable or schedule. Now, in this chapter, I am going to look more closely at how you use your time, and I think it will help you to fine tune and improve what should already be an effective part of your homeschooling life. I have made a list of seven simple things you can do with your timetable to increase your efficiency in your homeschooling.

1. DON'T BE A MAGPIE

Magpies collect bright shiny objects. They are always on the lookout for something new, something different and exciting. And homeschooling magpies are entranced by the advertising, the homeschool co-op chats, the shininess of the new book or shrink-wrapped box. The new product looks like it might solve any problems in homeschooling.

It might. But there is a good chance that it won't. It's more likely that no sooner have you set yourself up with the new system and approach to homeschooling, you will see something else which will be new, shiny, and full of promise.

Find something that works for you and stick with it—even if 'everyone else' is moving on to something shiny and new.

2. DON'T PUT TOO MANY THINGS IN YOUR TIMETABLE

When it comes to putting your timetable together, you may be tempted to think that the more subjects, the better. Not so. In fact, after about six—eight subjects, you will find that

There is no single RIGHT way to homeschool

productivity starts to decrease quite quickly. The vast number of subjects and the tightness of the schedule will actually discourage you, and you fall into the old, 'we're never going to get it all done, so why bother?' mind-set.

Then you end up not following your timetable at all, tackling the small, easy tasks (instead of the important things), or just giving up on it altogether. So that instead of keeping focus, gently guiding your children through the day in an orderly and kindly way, you may find yourself flying by the seat of your pants and handling whatever catches your attention. It's not the best way to make progress and teach good study habits to your little students.

The solution: Limit the number of subjects in your timetable and in particular, the number of trips out that you make each week.

You may be thinking, 'How on earth will I get through everything if I restrict the hours we work and the number of subjects we cover? The secret is to keep focused on the most important things you want to accomplish each week. And if you do manage to complete everything on your shorter timetable, and you have time and energy left over, you can always add a fun thing into your day.

If you're afraid that you might miss out an important part of your child's education, remember that you can ring the changes in some of the minor subjects, for example: covering a foreign language for one term and map drawing for another term.

If it seems as though other homeschoolers are covering much more interesting subjects than you are, don't berate yourself or try to add more into your busy day. Instead, make a note of the best of what you see others doing and when you plan your next block of time out, flick through these notes and choose any that you know will suit you and your children. In the meantime, keep your focus where it matters—on what is happening in your home with your children this week.

Just a week or two of using this method will show you how you actually can accomplish MORE by focusing on LESS. Give it a try; if it doesn't make you and the children more settled and productive, you can always go back to a full timetable. I think you'll find it was worth the experimentation. Remember to do what works for you.

3. FOLLOW YOUR TIMETABLE

When you have spent time putting together a roadmap to where you want to go, it's worthwhile actually following it. Every day will present its own problems and distractions, and you need to choose to follow your plan. Remember what you are doing, why you are doing it, where you want to go, and focus.

If you allow yourself to be distracted, sleep in, take extra time checking emails or browsing Facebook. If you decide to make muffins for morning tea, on a morning that you have already set aside for teaching a complicated mathematics lesson, or if you dawdle with household jobs until it's too late, on an afternoon set aside for getting paints out for an art lesson, then you won't accomplish your week's work with the children. And you won't end up with the results you wanted.

You also set the wrong example to your children who soon cotton on that if they can distract you with a squabble, a story, a 'good idea', or a million other things, they can wriggle out of anything they don't like the sound of.

The solution? It's easy: FOLLOW THE PLAN. When you have made your timetable, put the timetable in a prominent place and follow it. You don't have to think; you just have to move in the direction you're already pointed.

> 'A schedule defends from chaos and whim. It is a net for catching days. It is scaffolding on which a worker can stand and labour with both hands at sections of time.'
>
> ANNIE DILLARD

4. DON'T BECOME ENSLAVED TO YOUR TIMETABLE

Now, I've just told you about the importance of following your timetable. But some days, nothing seems to go as planned. The children get sick, the dog gets sick, YOU get sick. You can't control these occurrences. All you can do is do your best to move through them quickly and get back on track as soon as possible.

At other times, things can arise during the day that make it necessary to drop the timetable for an hour or two, or even a day or two.

You may be ready to read a chapter of the latest read-aloud and your youngest child vomits.

You have set aside a day to take the children on a visit to the zoo, but on the day, you are feeling sick, queasy, and tired.

Your sister who lives in another city and you haven't seen for a year is coming to visit you.

The weather is glorious after a week or two of rain—everyone needs to blow away the cobwebs, and you choose to get out and enjoy God's good earth and have a 'nature day'.

These sorts of events call for a change in the timetable. In fact, if it's something like a precious visitor, put the visit in your timetable. If you are pregnant and sleepy or with a new baby, allow time for your afternoon rest in your timetable.

Homeschooling can be so much fun, and one of your goals should be to enjoy homeschooling each day, as you live it. It's okay to set aside your timetable for special occasions—provided they're just that: special. If you find yourself dropping your timetable more than once a month, you need to take a look at your timetable and make adjustments. And if your timetable is fine, you may need to check if it's time for a proper rest and a week off.

But otherwise, try to enjoy the little break. You'll come back to your timetable the next day with renewed energy.

> *'There cannot be a crisis today; my schedule is already too full.'*
>
> HENRY KISSINGER

5. BE EFFECTIVE RATHER THAN PRODUCTIVE

It's easy to work through your daily timetable, reach the end of the day, and realise that while you got a lot of things done, you didn't do much to push your children towards your overall goals for them. Yes, you were all busy but you weren't effective.

It's easy to feel busy browsing online bookstores for homeschooling books or checking the library collection for some topic relevant to what you want to teach the children or tidying a toy shelf or sorting a drawer. You might even be able to fool yourself into thinking you're working (after all, you were sorting the homeschool stationery drawer, tidying the educational toys shelf and looking for homeschool books online). But at the end of the day—or week, or month—these activities will ensure that you haven't done with your children what you wanted to do.

Here are some questions to ask yourself to help determine if the tasks you're spending time on are busy work or real work:

- *Can someone else take care of this?* Can you ask one of the children to tidy that shelf on Saturday afternoon?
- *What would happen if I didn't do this?* Do you really need any more books on the subject of dinosaurs?
- *How much time do I typically spend doing this?* Checking email typically falls into this category. If you're checking your email five, ten, or more times per day, you may be avoiding your 'real' work of homeschooling.
- *Does this make me nervous?* Are you reluctant to have the mess of paints in the dining room for the morning? Are you unenthusiastic about the writing product you are using? If something on your timetable makes you a little anxious, work out why and what you are going to do about it.
- *Have I been avoiding doing this?* We tend to avoid tasks that make us feel uncomfortable (see the last point). If something has been continually pushed to the bottom of the list, then it might be the very thing you need to accomplish, today.

Once you wean yourself off the need to feel 'productive' and focus on becoming effective, instead, you'll notice a leap forward in how your children respond to your teaching and homeschooling in general.

6. LEARN FROM YOUR TIMETABLE

Timetables are dynamic documents. Today's timetable probably looks very different from one you made six months ago or a year ago (if it doesn't, it's time to revisit your goals). By looking back on previous timetables, you can learn a lot about yourself, your goals, and your habits—good and bad.

When you're finished with a timetable, don't throw it away. File it away and when you've got a year or two's worth of timetables stored up, pull them out and play detective. Ask yourself the following questions:

- What items have changed on my timetable? Why did they change?
- What has stayed the same? Are these things still there

because the children haven't learned those lessons yet, or have the actual lessons changed but the subject stayed. (e.g. maths will always be on the timetable.)
- What continually fails to appear on the timetable that should be there at least occasionally? This will help you see if you are avoiding something. Often it will be a subject that you don't like yourself, e.g. if you don't like messy crafts stuff or then it might not be on your timetable. If your children would like to try messy crafts you might look for a class to take them to.
- How many subjects do you typically have on the timetable, and how often do you complete the day's work, each day? Use this information as you move forward to make your current timetable more effective.
- How do you feel when you look back over your timetables? Are you struck with how much you've accomplished, or are you depressed by how much you never did? How can you use those feelings to motivate you now?
- In retrospect, were the items you thought were the most important turn out to really be the most important? If you had to do it over, would you place your emphasis, time, and resources elsewhere?

Your past timetables are valuable clues to your teaching and parenting style, preferences, and personality. Just as an archaeologist would review pieces of pottery and ancient artefacts for clues about that ancient civilization, you can review your own clues to make your present-day homeschooling effectiveness the highest it can be.

7. BE PREPARED

As well has having an effective timetable, it's important that you also feel prepared each day and each week, ahead of time.

Some people might like to give the children Friday afternoon extra time to play and then spend an hour on preparing for the following week.

Make your to-do list each evening, in preparation for the next day. This skill is critical to your success. Sitting down for fifteen minutes to plan out the next day before you turn the page on the calendar increases your effectiveness for several reasons:

- Your unconscious mind starts working on the things you need to do before you even wake up in the morning.
- You can hit the ground running, without distractions. If you don't know where you're going, it's really easy to get pulled off track—you mess around, checking email, returning phone calls, texting, and wondering what you might have for lunch. Before you know it, half the day is gone, and you haven't done anything.
- Your to-do list coupled with your timetable keeps you focused. You won't get side-tracked by the unimportant that hits your inbox or voicemail because you already know where you're heading.
- Writing a to-do list provides closure to your day. It will be easier to stop thinking about homeschooling when you know you've taken care of all the loose ends and are primed to start the next day.

After you get in the habit of ending your day with making your next day's to-do list, you'll soon find the exercise a relaxing and encouraging way to close out. If you've accomplished great things with the children, you can pat yourself on the back and gear up for more. If today was less than stellar, you can get re-energised for the day to come. In either case, it'll help you sleep better at night.

> *'I'm not busy ... a woman with three children under the age of ten wouldn't think my schedule looks so busy.'*
>
> GARRISON KEILLOR

SUMMARY

Today's chapter has been all about perfecting, refining, and improving what is already a successful homeschool. Fine-tuning will be a part of your regular homeschool lifestyle, as you have done today.

ASSIGNMENT

Choose one of the seven refinements from today's chapter and apply it over the coming week.

CHAPTER 23
START AND END IN A SPECIAL WAY

Now that you are settled into homeschooling I want to address the issue of where schools do better than homeschool.

There are so few of these things that they hardly count, but one of them is the ability of schools to celebrate as a community. To celebrate successes and to show off how good they are with exam results, performances, sports teams, etc.

For homeschoolers, our children can belong to sports teams and participate in performances reasonably easily. Exam results are just that—exam results. If we are focused on learning, as opposed to achieving, then exam results will be low priority for most of the time.

But what about the aspect of celebrating success and achievements ? I have some ideas to help you on this.

The beginning of a school year has a great sense of newness and 'fresh start'. And the same for the end of the year when things start to wind down as everything heads towards a finale. Children have exams or assessments and school reports. People start to plan holidays, and there is a general frenzy of anticipation.

Obviously, this doesn't happen in homeschooling families to the same degree. But that doesn't mean you can't celebrate it means that you just celebrate in different ways.

In fact, not only is it possible to celebrate, I think that it's an integral and absolutely vital part of homeschooling to celebrate milestones, achievements, and the marking of seasons.

START THE YEAR RIGHT
There are various ways to mark the start of the year.
1. Start the year a bit later than the schools. This means that you have a lovely quiet time in late summer, when everywhere is a bit quieter, the frenzy of summer holidays is over, and you can enjoy peaceful summer activities without the rush.

2. Allow some days before the beginning of the year to get yourself organised, make plans, etc. Schools do this; they call these days 'Teacher Only Days'. So have a few 'Teacher Only Days'. Then when you do start, you can start in a peaceful and orderly way.
3. Make a date to start and mark the calendar, so that everyone can look forward to it.
4. Take a photograph of your children in the first week of the school year. Do this every year. It will act as a reminder of how the children are growing and put milestones in your homeschooling life.
5. On the very first morning of the term, I like to do something very special. You can maybe go out for breakfast or pack a picnic and go out for a long walk. Choose something completely different and wonderful. It generates so much good will and pleasure and excitement with the children. And it really makes them feel special.
6. If your children are ten or over, involve them in planning the timetable. Ask them what they would like to study, get them to make lists, and try and incorporate some of their list into the timetable.
7. For your first art lesson of the year, get the children to design a poster with a motto for themselves for the year. For example, in 2021, a motto might be: 'Get Things Done in Twenty-one'. If your child is working on having a good attitude, his motto might be, 'Settle Down Without a Frown'.
8. Make sure your timetable and motto posters are displayed attractively by the end of the first week.

END THE YEAR WELL

The end of the year often includes some homeschooling events that you will be involved with. Try to invite extended family if it's suitable. This can often sway the most sceptical of grandfathers in favour of homeschooling, when he sees the children producing beautiful work of some sort, be it an exhibition, concert, show or display.

But your family will also want to acknowledge a year of hard work and wonderful progress. One way to do this is with an end of year letter.

THE LETTER

- Every year, in place of a report, you can write each child a letter.
- List their learning experiences, achievements, and moments of glory.
- Be as creative and inventive as you like.
- Use your diary and planner to remind yourself of what you child has actually done throughout the year.
- You can work through your child's efforts either chronologically or by subject. If you choose to work chronologically, you might have sections like this: 'In March you...' And if you choose to work by subject you might have sections like this: 'For History this year you...'
- Illustrate your child's letter with photographs of your child and his work.
- Tell your child what aspect of his learning and his character you are particularly pleased with this year.
- You can mention things that you are looking forward to doing next year with your child.
- Don't be surprised if your letter is several pages long
- Print your letter in colour, on beautiful paper.
- If possible, have both parents sign the letter. This really matters to the children.
- Have a beautiful, decorated envelope for the letter.

PRESENTING THE LETTER

- The presentation of the letter is quite important so don't rush this part.
- Arrange a special morning tea or dinner.
- Put on nice clothes and have special food. This makes your child feel valued and gives a sense of occasion to the event.
- Invite extended family and some friends if at all possible.
- Consider joining with one or two other close homeschool families if that suits.
- Make a fuss of presenting the letter to your child.
- Finally, enjoy the yummies that you have prepared beforehand.

DURING THE HOLIDAYS

It's a well-known fact that children lose a lot of ground in learning when they take a long summer holiday. I recommend that you have a maintenance plan to just keep your child's hand in.

- Set aside an hour or two a week for maintenance.
- Maintenance will include some sort of pencil work E.g. maybe your child will write a letter or a diary once a week and draw a picture.
- If your child is a new reader, get him to read a couple of sentences a day to you, so that he doesn't forget all he has learned.
- If he is a strong reader, ensure that he always has a book to read.
- Holiday time is a good time for lighter reading, for example, the Tin Tin books and Asterix.
- Keep up some library visits during the holidays
- Make sure you have a break yourself, it's your holiday too.

SUMMARY

In this chapter you have learnt:
- How to start and end the year in style.
- How to use these occasions to motivate, inspire and encourage your children.
- How to feel good about the valuable work you do as a homeschooling parent.

ASSIGNMENT

- Consider what you want to do to make your own start and finish times special.
- Discuss this with any significant adults in your family who are likely to be involved.
- Make notes in your planner or diary for two weeks before the start of finish of term, to remind yourself to prepare for the celebration.

CHAPTER 24
LOOK HOW FAR YOU'VE COME!

Over the past few months you have hopefully been reading a chapter a week, and applying what you are learning, so that this book is really helping and guiding you in your homeschooling.

At the start of this book I told you that if you followed the recommendations in the book you would be fireproofed against burnout. And that's true.

If things start to feel hard, it's time to step back, take a breath, pull out this book and your notes, and reassess things. Read your notes carefully. Remember why you are doing this, what is important, and why it's important to you.

Make adjustments as you need to. Fine tune things in the areas where you're not feeling comfortable. Keep a good perspective on the whole area of homeschooling in your family. It's not the be all and end all of life. It's not even the be all and end all of your daily life today. It's a way of living, a part of your life.

So take a break, have a 'reading week' or an 'outdoors week' and allow more freedom for yourself and your children while you spend time reassessing and refocusing.

Then, when you are refocused and refreshed, you can come back to homeschooling, with renewed vigour, and you never even got to burnout.

IN THIS BOOK, WE HAVE COVERED:
- How to start homeschooling today.
- Literacy hour.
- Mathematics hour.
- Bringing your children out of school.
- How to develop a good vision.
- How to work out your goals.
- How to fireproof your homeschool.
- How to fulfil your own dreams.

- How to work out what curriculum will suit you.
- How to decide how often you will go out during the week.
- How to keep your home clean and tidy while homeschooling.
- Making a workable, practical timetable
- Working with the ebb and flow of life.
- Record keeping.
- How to make a visit to the library into a highlight of your week.
- Writing a lesson plan.
- Teaching science.
- Avoiding homeschool burnout.
- What veteran homeschoolers would do differently
- Dealing with clutter.
- Keeping your family safe online.
- A fun homeschooling quiz.
- Seven simple things you can do to be more efficient in homeschool.
- Beginnings and endings: make them special.

WHERE TO FROM HERE?

Now that you have completed this book with me, you are well and truly settled in homeschooling, but you won't stop learning about homeschooling. Opportunities will come up all the time, and an attitude of having a lifestyle of learning is what makes it all so much fun.

Have you looked at *Charlotte Mason Made Easy*? 'Charlotte Mason Education' is the fastest-growing movement in home education today, and with good reason. There is so much of Charlotte Mason's philosophy which suits modern homeschoolers.

www.CharlotteMasonMadeEasy.com

Also, you might be interested in teaching English grammar to your children in an easy, and fun way. A way that will help your children remember parts of speech, how to use punctuation, and tricky spellings.

www.GrammarLessonsMadeEasy.co.nz

LAST PIECE OF ADVICE

I have one final piece of advice for you. If you only take from this book one thing, let it be this. Do this before anything and everything else:

ENJOY YOUR CHILDREN

Your children are not with you forever, and they will soon grow up and leave home to forge their own lives as adults. Your job is to prepare them for adult life and to work yourself out of a job. A couple of thoughts about enjoying your children and keeping perspective in your homeschooling journey:
- Don't be overemotional and sentimental with your children.
- Don't avoid discipline because you want your children like you.
- Don't spoil your children in an attempt to create 'happy families'.
- Don't try to create memories for your children, create memories for yourself.
- Do remember that you are not your children's 'friend', you are their loving parent.
- Do remember that you're the grown-up, so you lead the way in being kind, fair and mature.
- Do enjoy the moment, enjoy the teaching, enjoy watching your child grow and learn, enjoy life in your own family.

And don't forget—the days pass slowly but the years pass quickly.

ABOUT THE AUTHOR

Stephanie Walmsley is a teacher by profession, with classroom teaching experience in New Zealand and England. She and her husband, Philip, started officially homeschooling their five children in January 1985. The older two had a couple of spells in school; the younger three never went to school.

She worked as a volunteer for over twenty years, supporting mothers in their mothering and homeschooling. Then in 2002 she started writing and conducting courses for homeschooling parents because she saw a need for good, professional, homeschool help available from someone who has 'walked the talk'.

She has written a series of online courses for homeschooling mothers, and also has eBooks and study guides available.

Her passion is to support parents with their children and especially in their home education.

Visit Stephanie at www.successfulhomeschoolingmadeeasy.com

www.ingramcontent.com/pod-product-compliance
Lightning Source LLC
Chambersburg PA
CBHW021438080526
44588CB00009B/578